GNARR

GNARR

How I Became the Mayor of a Large
City in Iceland and Changed the World

JÓN GNARR

Translated by Andrew Brown

MELVILLE HOUSE
BROOKLYN · LONDON

GNARR

Translation copyright © 2014 by Andrew Brown

First Melville House Printing: June 2014

First published in German under the title
*Hören Sie gut zu und wiederholen Sie!!!: Wie ich einmal
Bürgermeister wurde und die Welt veränderte* by
Jón Gnarr, with the collaboration of
Jóhann Ævar Grímsson

Melville House Publishing   8 Blackstock Mews
          145 Plymouth Street   and   Islington
          Brooklyn, NY 11201   London N4 2BT

mhpbooks.com   facebook.com/mhpbooks   @melvillehouse

ISBN: 978-1-61219-413-4

Library of Congress Control Number: 2014941720

Manufactured in the United States of America
1 3 5 7 9 10 8 6 4 2

CONTENTS

INTRODUCTION

Theories are clever things. In politics there are a lot of theories that make perfect sense: socialism, with its classless society, equality, and fraternity; or liberalism, which wants to give everyone enough leeway to work freely. Even in education and culture, there are smart ideas. And in the different religions. But unfortunately there is something to which no theory is immune: human weakness. Immaturity is one weakness. Selfishness another. Greed. No matter what ideology you hold to, sooner or later greed and selfishness get in the way, especially when it comes to human encounters.

In partnerships and families, at school or at work. Wherever people are trying to build something up, a single individual can bring everything crashing down. We know this from apartment buildings. You only need one person to step out of line and things get out of hand. In an apartment building, there are usually a few regulations about the use of laundry rooms and detergents. As long as everyone follows the rules, it all works beautifully. But there's always someone who doesn't seem able to do so. We've all met these people: the neighbors who leave their laundry hanging in the laundry room for days on end or use all of your detergent without asking. That's the kind of thing that undermines the whole system. If we all try just a little bit to keep that from happening, I think we might not need any rules.

I've always divided people into two categories. There are the givers, the big-hearted people who assume responsibility and don't leave any litter, in either the everyday or the more spiritual sense. And then there are the others, the people who don't yield an inch because for some reason they can't or won't, perhaps because they think everyone else owes them something. They're always quick to accept the help of others, but the idea of actually offering help themselves never seems to occur to them. These people are spiritual bloodsuckers.

I've been dragging this problem around with me my whole life, and I'm pretty used to dividing people into "givers" and "takers." I feel good when I'm dealing with people who give me something, especially when it's joy they give me. I'm particularly grateful for people who surprise me—those who have something beautiful, funny, or perplexing up their sleeves and conjure it up without expecting anything definite in return. And also those who simply give me a present—whereupon, I try to do the same.

In 2008, Iceland experienced the terrible consequences of the economic crisis. The country's banks crashed in a catastrophic way, and we soon learned that the government had practiced no oversight of our banks whatsoever, with cronyism and incompetence at work at the highest legislative levels. The forces that brought about the economic collapse were selfishness and greed: the bankers made risky investments, enriched themselves, they bought big houses and fancy cars, and then all of the economic miracles of the Icelandic banking economy were exposed as fiction. The rest of the country suffered. Huge protests, directed at the government and the banks, soon followed.

As I detail in these pages, my response to the crisis was somewhat different: in 2009, I founded a political party with my friends: The Best Party.

In 2010, the party ran in the Reykjavík city council election. We won six of the fifteen seats, which meant that—after we formed a coalition government—I became mayor of Reykjavík, the capital of Iceland and the only big city in the country, home to most of Iceland's citizens, as well as its government, banks, and thriving arts community.

When I entered politics I freely called myself an anarchist. But does that mean I seriously think that the dream of an ideal society in which everyone takes care of everyone else and everyone respects the rights of others can actually come true? A society in which you don't need any rules, because everyone is so kind and mature and intelligent? No, I don't think so.

When it came to democracy and politics, I had tended up until then to go for a comfy, rather passive attitude. The Best Party was my first attempt at getting involved. When I created the Best Party, I made a point of bringing in as many generous, intelligent, and sincere people as I could identify. Most of these people had, like so many others of the same ilk, ended up following the route of passivity in politics. With the Best Party I wanted to address precisely these people and get them to join in. I encouraged them to get involved in a positive way—even though the gibe that "the anarchist is one who criticizes society from the comfort of his armchair" also applies, unfortunately, to myself.

Leo Tolstoy once said, "Everyone wants to change the world, but no one wants to change himself." But I feel that I have changed myself. I've done my homework. And next I want to try—just try, mind you!—to change the world. In a positive way. This essentially means leading by example. The Best Party wants to be a good example. We strive for honesty. We are against violence. And where others see problems, we provide solutions. All this is extremely tiring, but it's what we've tried to do.

This book is an attempt to tell the story of my own political evolution and how I came to form the Best Party.

I'm often asked what I am particularly proud of in my party's work. Of course, we've achieved a lot. Since my election as mayor of Reykjavík, we've created cycle paths, organized funding for social projects, redesigned urban areas, and supported new works of art for public spaces. But what I'm really proud of, to be honest, is just the fact that we still exist. I'm proud that a group of people from outside the political class has come together to try and change things, and has stuck with this ambitious project. We're still here, and still with the original cast. We've also encouraged many young people to open their mouths and intervene wherever something strikes them as unjust, wrong, or pointless. I can well imagine, at least I hope, that our actions and methods will provide a lesson.

GNARR

THE FUTURE

A manifesto by Jón Gnarr, posted January 12, 2010, on the website of the Best Party.

Recently I was traveling abroad and suddenly felt the urge to pop into a swimming pool. I headed off to a kind of spa resort where I expected to find a pool, but—zilch. Instead, there were only a couple of hot tubs, and they weren't even particularly hot. Still, there was a Jacuzzi bubbling away, so I gave it a try. Apart from me there was only one other bather present, an old man. I gave him a brief nod as I stepped into the water, then I closed my eyes and let the air bubbles rinse all the stress from my body. Suddenly the old man spoke to me.

"What do you think the future holds for Iceland?" he asked.

I was speechless. "I *am* from Iceland," I finally replied. He didn't reply and let his eyelids droop again. Did he know that I was an Icelander? And if so, *how* could he know? Only when we said goodbye in the parking lot did I notice that he had a special issue of the local paper—in which I had been profiled—in his sports bag.

The man was Knut Finkelstein, a futurologist from Frankfurt, Germany, who'd been fascinated by my interview in the paper and, like many other readers in Frankfurt at the time, apparently, was really worried about the future of Iceland.

On my foreign trips I often chat with children and teenagers. They too all seem to take a passionate interest in Iceland; many have read interviews and want to find out everything they can about the Best Party. I'm always very touched when I have a crowd of these young people around me, as they really seem to be deeply affected, blown away really, by all the things happening around them.

In Iceland, I recently visited a small village out in the country. There I met a tourist who told me proudly how he'd once eaten Icelandic lamb on a vacation through the United States. I was delighted to hear it, of course. Coincidentally, I had a big bottle of cocktail sauce in my bag, and I pressed it into his hand when we said goodbye. "Next time you have Icelandic lamb, dip it in this!"

Eventually the only cars around will be electric ones. And there'll be batteries that last much longer than today. And Christmas tree ornaments that light up all by themselves. The people in power never think that far ahead. This is not good. They drift helplessly forward, bobbing along like someone clinging on to a weather balloon he's lost control of. These are the people who call the shots in our country. When it comes to planning for the future, the authorities have failed to adopt a clear course that everyone can live with. Basically, they don't give a damn about the future, as they think it's completely irrelevant. So far, not a single member of Parliament in Iceland has had the courage to openly and honestly address the important questions about the future. No other party considers a programmatic look into the future as one of its values.

We do! We could certainly look forward to a rosy future—if people would only vote for us. If not, I'm afraid the outlook is dark. Everyone's heart will sink down into his boots. Everything will be privatized, while the state nonetheless keeps it all under its thumb. Beer will be illegal again, just like being gay or driving a car. The EU will swallow us entirely and force us to give up everything we hold dear—such as fermented mutton testicles and smoked lamb. There's no way to resist. If we put up a fight, Brussels will send troops to Iceland to shoot on sight anyone who violates EU rules. They'll haul people out of their houses and shoot them down in the middle of the street—just because they've put too much salt on their food perhaps, or taken a pinch of snuff. Neoliberalism in all its pomp and splendor will make its triumphant entry, and sooner or later everything will be up for sale: we'll have a society that lies somewhere between economic liberalism and the nanny state. Eventually, people will even sell off their own organs just to afford a bit of luxury. What can you really call your own when you have to sell a kidney in order to celebrate your birthday? Nothing. And everyone's wearing the same clothes.

The other day I dreamed of the future. I was at a meeting with some high-ranking politicians. The main Icelandic ministers were there, but also Hitler, Mahatma Gandhi, and Chuck Norris, and these people were apparently now going to govern our country. What happened then I don't know, except that all at once I had supernatural powers, as in *The Matrix*, and could walk through walls. In another dream I watched while, somewhere like the Austurvöllur in the city center of Reykjavík, children were being sacrificed to appease the shareholders. And all the old established politicians came to enjoy the children's blood. The prime minister slurped so greedily that blood ran down from the corners of her mouth and seeped into her blouse, the finance minister was gnawing on a human bone, and Idi Amin had come to join them. The bystanders wept.

That's a bleak scenario for the future. Do we want such a future for our children? Do we want them to be swallowed wholesale? The Best Party certainly doesn't. We have an appointment with the future, and we're going to meet it like a new friend, at first hesitantly and timidly, then more and more confidently and expectantly. In the society of the future, as we see it, everyone is happy and contented, uses free buses and swimming pools, and talks over all the reasons why the Best Party is so good. Disease, grief, and pain are things of the past. Nobody ever dies, they all live on, and if they need money, they just go into the nearest bank and have some printed—free of charge, of course. Anyway, money is now only of use as decoration or as a toy to play with. Because if we can turn our concept into reality, everything will be free. May we invite you to make a date with this rosy future? Then put your cross in the box marked *Best Party*.

ICELAND

Iceland appears on old maps as an island "beyond the habitable world." Sailors warned you not to take a course to this Devil's Island, because, on the old maps, the sea route to Iceland swarmed with sea monsters. When the ancient Greeks came this way, they quickly realized that there was nothing here, either for them or for anyone else.

People have tried to find a reason for the name "Iceland" for as long as anyone can remember. Some, for example, support the theory that the names "Greenland" and "Iceland" somehow got confused in hoary antiquity. Iceland is rather a green island. In no other country in the world do so many moss and lichen species grow as here, while in Greenland there's not a single blade of grass to be seen far and wide.

But it is interesting that the prefix *ice-* in the Romance languages doesn't have anything to do with the substance ice: it's linked to *island*, being derived from the Latin word *insula* or *isola*. My own theory is that it might have come about this way: When the first Vikings set out on their raids into the northern seas, they must have come across a map belonging to Christian monks on which Iceland was indeed shown, but was simply named *Insula*. But the ancient Norsemen, who weren't too great at foreign languages, couldn't make heads or tails of this, and so did their own number on it; they changed the letters, added the ending "-and," and lo and behold: it made sense. I don't find this explanation all that far-fetched.

All Icelanders go swimming. It's one of the undisputed advantages of this country that just about anywhere you go has a marvelously well-equipped swimming pool nearby. Icelandic pools are more than just swimming pools. They are complete spas with saunas, hot tubs, massage facilities, and solaria. The swimming pools are maintained by the local councils and seen as a basic service. Town councils are even obliged to allow their citizens reasonably priced access. If actual socialism has really found a niche anywhere in Iceland, it's in the swimming pools.

In the pools, it's just like in the phone book, everyone's the same. In the hot tubs, which have always been very relaxed, bank directors and harbor workers sit together in the hot water and discuss politics and current events. Extra pools for the elite just don't exist. The rich splash about in the same tank as the common folk. Outside, you look at people and you can see what social class they come from, you can read from their clothing and appearance how much they earn. In an Icelandic hot tub you can forget all that. The stocky bald guy next to you might be a very rich ship owner with four lovers at once, and the sensitive young man opposite, who you'd spontaneously typecast as a philosopher or poet, could equally well be a shoemaker. Everyone pulls off their clothes and works up a nice lather in the shower in front of everyone else. This makes you more modest.

To understand Iceland, you have to go to the pool. It's the swimming pools that forge us into a nation, more than anything else I think.

Despite what you may have heard, our solidarity with the Norwegians, Danes, and Swedes has its limits. We don't feel particularly close to the mainland Scandinavians, although the first settlers in Iceland came from precisely these countries. Instead, we feel in some mysterious way attracted to the Finns. Icelanders often like to emphasize how "Icelandic" the Finns are, and the Finns willingly return the compliment: they find us pretty "Finnish"—just as relaxed, awkward, and depressed. This secret bond between Finns and Icelanders must have something to do with the Finnish sauna culture. You see, the Finns are, just like us, a naked people. In Finland, it's the most natural thing in the world to wander around stark naked in front of strangers, without feeling ashamed of your body or the bodies of others.

In Icelandic swimming pools you can regularly see foreign visitors who find this unabashed nakedness strange. The tourists wrap themselves up tightly in their towels before coyly discarding their underwear and getting into their swimsuits. These inhibitions always amuse us Icelanders—while we, with our towels thrown casually over our shoulders, let our freshly showered breasts or dicks cheerfully dangle as we stroll around.

As long as I can remember, in Iceland it was all pretty straightforward. Here, strictly speaking, nothing happens. The country has just 320,000 people, so if someone falls off his bike, it's worth at least a headline in the daily paper. If celebrities from abroad come to visit, they often emphasize how enjoyable and relaxing life is with us—in contrast to the grotesque media circus that springs up around them everywhere else. There are no tabloids and no paparazzi.

The most famous Icelander is Björk. Despite everything, she's always remained herself. Abroad, she constantly has to flee from fans and journalists who pursue her into every little corner, while in Iceland you run into her in the pool, on the bus, or in the shops. In general, she's left alone.

In Iceland I was famous by the time I was fourteen. I was a fourteen-year-old with a Mohawk and a ring through his nose, and this too was news. By the time I was thirty, and earned my living as a comedian and actor, almost every child in Iceland knew me. Whenever I was appearing in some television series, the city was filled with huge advertising posters with a picture of me on the walls of the houses. And when I got onto a bus, it was quite likely that the bus would be running ads for me too.

It was quite a sensation if somewhere or other some elderly guy *didn't* know who I was. Once, somebody told me about one such old timer who in all seriousness had never heard of me—this aroused laughter from those standing around. As you can see, being famous is different in Iceland from what it is elsewhere. In Iceland, everything is boringly normal. Even celebrity. People know that before you go swimming, you stand there naked in the shower just like they do.

The only practical use of celebrity is that it sometimes saves you having to queue for the clubs on the weekends. But at clubs, like everywhere else, you'll most likely have to join the line like all the other well-behaved folk. Even Björk joins the line at the end and waits until it's her turn, and everyone finds this normal. Sometimes a bouncer decides to show her preferential treatment, but the bystanders find this misplaced and awkward.

The Icelandic state of mind is dominated by the seasons. Summer is the best time. On the "first day of summer" (which according to the calendar is the third Thursday in April), we all wish each other "Have a great summer!" This is a nice custom. In summer, everyone is happy. There's hardly an Icelandic poet who hasn't, sooner or later, sung about our summer, our wonderful summer, which is so much better than any other summer in the world. Although not all that much better, actually.

We have to use the power of positive thinking, to enjoy the half-full glass. The thermometer rarely manages more than 20 degrees Celsius (68°F), but the minute it hits ten degrees (50°F), we pull all our clothes off. Temperatures much above this are considered a heat wave. In summertime, the living is easy. And when someone indulges in pessimism, we just turn a deaf ear. Everyone's optimistic and cheerful, we're the happiest people under the sun—because it's summer.

With the fall, comes fear. The days get shorter and the nights, as a result, longer. Suddenly our worries are back. We wonder whether it's going to be a hard winter.

When winter comes, we stick our heads under the duvet. Now is the time to stay at home. There's not much energy left for winter romances in this country. Not only do we not have any real summer, but no real winter either. If it snows one day, there's a frost the next day and on the third day it rains. The lakes are frozen in the morning and thawed again in the evening. You never know what to expect. That's why, unlike the other Scandinavians, we Icelanders have never made much headway in the winter sports. The only sport we're really good at is chess. After all, indoors you can hunker down at the chessboard all year round.

We are shaped through and through by nature and the elements. We have a tremendous ability to adapt—and you need plenty of that if you want to survive in this country. You can never rely on everything staying the way it was here. The earth might quake or a volcano could erupt. Your garden might get buried under a lava flow, and there are snow storms in June. But we've learned to live with it—perhaps because we've maintained a certain degree of humility towards nature and her moods.

Nature we cannot change, but we *can* change ourselves and our way of thinking. To nature we can only adapt. We go fishing when the sun shines and we make hay when the sun shines. This adaptability has always been our strength, as it's the only way to survive here. If you don't make an effort, don't store provisions, and don't use the opportunities that present themselves to you, then when winter comes you'll simply starve.

SEND IN THE CLOWN

I was born into a working-class family in Iceland. We lived in a Reykjavík suburb on a street called Kurland, named after a Norwegian village. My parents were ordinary folk. My mother worked in a hospital canteen and my father was a policeman, but he never got very far in his career because of his Communist views.

By the time I happened along, my parents were no longer spring chickens. According to a frequently cited family anecdote, I was supposedly the result of a drunken, day-bright May night in the West Fjords, maybe even the night of the First of May—for my father, one of the holiest days of the year. The late pregnancy was a huge shock for my parents, not least for Mom, who was terribly ashamed to be producing me at the age of forty-five. Dad was fifty.

When I finally arrived in the world, I turned out to be a redhead, which raised all sorts of questions. Dad's hair was raven black. My grandmother, who lived with us, was convinced that the father of the baby just *had* to be our next-door neighbor . . .

My brothers and sisters were all much older than

me, and in my childhood I had little or nothing to do with them. It was my parents, my two grandmothers, and my aunts and uncles who brought me up. My parents' siblings were older than them, and every year an uncle or aunt died. Someone was always dying. Most of them got cancer and slowly wasted away, and at some point in the midst of all this death, both grandmothers died too.

I was considered to be difficult. Wild and impetuous, with a short attention span, I put up resistance to everything and everyone. I did, however, learn to talk extremely early and by the time I was just two I was chattering freely. I tended to hide myself away instead of playing with other children, but then again I was untamable, climbed trees and house roofs, ran out into the street, and put my safety at risk in all sorts of independent ways. I also liked throwing bad language around, the more indecent the better. I was a permanent provocation, and never predictable.

So right from the start I was seen as the black sheep of the family. I was a precocious child in a deadlocked world. My allegedly abnormal behavior was the normal reaction to abnormal circumstances. As is so often the case. The neighbors pretty much all thought there was something seriously wrong with me and doubted that I would ever cope in a normal school. After my umpteenth trip to the emergency room, they sent my mother and me to a child and adolescent psychiatrist, who, after thoroughly examining and evaluating me for over a year, diagnosed me as *maladaptio*. To many, it was just a fancy word for "retarded."

By chance, there was in our district a school where a kind of pilot project was being tested out: lessons without the usual classes and awarding of grades. They worked on the so-called "open education" system, then a very revolutionary concept. In this school, I felt comfortable. In class, I behaved as conspicuously as possible, getting up to all sorts of mischief and raising a rumpus whenever I could. But that was okay. They took me as I was and treated me with respect, consideration, and patience. To begin with, I even performed exceptionally well with the curriculum. Reading in particular fascinated me, and soon I was reading everything I could lay my hands on, whether for children or adults, comics or non-fiction.

In reading, general knowledge, and telling stories I was one of the best, but when it came to writing and arithmetic, I was worse than mediocre. My letters were either upside down or back to front, my spelling was haphazard, and it was impossible for me to fit the words neatly on a line. The letters I wrote home on summer vacation were often passed around at family gatherings, where they were a reliable source of amusement. I was fifteen before I could really write.

I realized at a young age that I wasn't cut out for everyday life at school. I still had the impression I was learning lots of useful things in the classroom because it helped me get a handle on everything I overheard on TV or read in books, but what the teachers taught us was rarely what really mattered. This insight grew with each passing year, and when I was eleven I just refused to go on learning school stuff. I'd had enough of the one-sided pedagogy and the soulless knowledge that school wanted to impose on me.

For example, I refused point-blank to learn Danish. I could see no practical use for this language. I would much rather have learned English, but unfortunately that wasn't taught. Or why not Norwegian? I had a sister in Norway, I could visit her and at least make myself understood.

Mathematics was another subject I wasn't all that good at. I knew that I'd never be brilliant at it, and I found it more reasonable to concentrate on what I was good at, rather than slogging my guts out to no purpose. Also, I've always been allergic to repetition. If I ever have to repeat the same thing over and over, I get so panicky and anxious that I can hardly breathe. That's also why I've not appeared onstage as an actor much. After the endless rehearsals, the play hangs round my neck like an albatross and I can barely force myself to play the role on stage. Even for the premiere I have to make a real effort.

So I announced at home that I wasn't doing any more schoolwork. Instead, I'd watch TV or read. This led to lengthy discussions between me, my mother, the teachers, and the headmaster.

"If you don't learn anything, you'll be a nobody.

What are you going to be when you grow up? A garbage man, perhaps?" they said.

The idea was certainly tempting. Garbage men were the pirates of the modern era. They came at dawn, casually jumping onto the backs of their garbage trucks. They were free and independent. Whistling and cheerfully yelling out to one another, they swooped down on the trashcans and then, just as suddenly as they had appeared, vanished. For me, the garbage men were like heroes, and I looked up to them with admiration.

THE POLITICS OF MY YOUTH

My father was a political man through and through. Politics always played a central role in our home. When visitors came, the conversation was mainly about politics. When there was something about politics on the radio or television, the volume was immediately turned up. I tried to understand what was going on, but found such issues extremely boring.

In our home, the political world was divided into two parts: Left and Right. Mom didn't have a great deal to do with politics. She voted for Sjálfstæðisflokkurinn, the Independence Party, the largest and oldest right-wing party in Iceland, but she refused to discuss it or to talk about politics at all. Dad, as I mentioned, was a Communist. He had been a member of the Communist Party of Iceland when it still existed, and his political orientation put its stamp on every aspect of our family life. Dad was a reliable, punctual, and efficient police officer in Reykjavík, but self-confessed Communists had very limited opportunities for advancement in the police force. That's why he remained a mere traffic cop throughout his life, while his colleagues worked their ways up the career ladder step-by-step.

He thought highly of the Soviet Union, was a

member of the Icelandic and Soviet Russian Cultural Association, and subscribed to a magazine called *Soviet News*. Whenever there were personnel changes in the Politburo of the Soviet Union, Dad was sent a framed photo of the new arrival to display at home. I remember how he passed on to Mom and me all of Brezhnev's announcements. The only time of day we all met was the evening meal. When Brezhnev had said something worth noting, Dad took this opportunity to tell us about it. Neither Mom nor I were particularly gagging to find out what Brezhnev had said or done, but we kept quiet and nodded, looking interested.

Brezhnev was hanging on the wall in our pantry—on a photo, under glass. He looked grim, wore a kind of uniform, and was bedecked with all sorts of decorations and medals. In 1982, Yuri Andropov took over the office of Secretary General, and Dad got a photo of him too. Andropov did not look all that different from Brezhnev, except that he had fewer medals on his chest. Dad, proud and happy, wandered round the apartment with the photo and wanted to hang it up somewhere straightaway. But Mom wouldn't hear of it. Dad continued to search for a suitable place, but Mom was adamant. Andropov wouldn't have suited either our living room or the kitchen or the TV room, and so he ended up in the pantry next to his predecessor.

Mom and Dad subscribed to two daily newspapers: the right-wing *Morgunblaðið* and the left-liberal *Þjóðviljinn*. The pages of these newspapers accurately reflected the Cold War, as both of them commented on the day's events from their particular perspective. The political leaders were either gods or the spawn of the Devil.

I myself subscribed to two magazines, *Donald Duck* and *Youth*, an Icelandic Christian magazine for children and teenagers, but both appeared only once a month. I studied each issue with great care, from beginning to end, hoping to come across something interesting. And if I already knew the current issue of *Donald Duck* by heart, I also grabbed the *Soviet News*—just to provide myself with reading material—which then kept me up to speed on those wonderful brand-new tractors that had been delivered to some Soviet farm.

Thanks to Dad, the newspapers, and the constant discussions broadcast on radio and television, I developed an aversion to politics. Politics was dumb, irritating, and boring. And unfair, too: just because the United States and the Soviet Union couldn't agree, we all lived on a powder keg. The Soviets had their nuclear missiles aimed at America, and American missiles were aimed at the Soviet Union. It was only a matter of time before nuclear war broke out. In principle, it could happen at any moment. The consequences for the world would be devastating and would wipe out all human life on Earth forever. In my youthful innocence I often thought that the world would definitely be more peaceful and beautiful if people would just leave politics alone. If they'd just drop all the political drivel and talk about other issues, such as pirates, food, or garbage men.

PUNK

I was thirteen when I discovered punk. At that time it was quite difficult in Iceland to find out anything about punk. All we had was a single legal radio station that was limited to Icelandic choral and classical music. Often the pieces and their interpreters were not even identified, there was just a quick standard intro saying, "And now for a few cheerful bars from our record library." Punk rarely, if ever, cropped up in the Icelandic media, and the music on offer was so limited that we mainly consumed it in the form of cassettes that we listened to over and over again. In the library there was *Melody Maker*—the weekly British music newspaper—and in the bookstores the German teen magazine *Bravo*.

I have no idea why *Bravo* was sold here, but I could always find articles about punk in it. Because I didn't know any German, I had to rely on the pictures. Once I managed to get my hands on an issue with a poster of Nina Hagen, the German punk singer. I pinned the poster up on the wall of my room straightaway. Nina Hagen was my first great love: I had a hopeless crush on her. Until I heard her sing for the first time. What a disappointment! Either she mumbled in German, or suddenly started caterwauling an opera number.

Punk and opera just didn't go together, in my view. Also, I couldn't understand her lyrics at all. The only thing I seemed to gather from listening was that she wanted to go to Africa. And what was punk about that? Were there even any punks in Africa? Wouldn't she have done much better in England?

It was the Sex Pistols who brought me close to punk. This mainly had to do with the fact that Johnny Rotten was a redhead just like me. I wanted to resemble him in every way. This went so far that I for a time gave myself the stage name "Jónsi Rotten," scribbled it in all my textbooks, and daubed the walls of houses with it.

Then I came across Crass, the British punk band that promoted anarchism, and everything else was overshadowed. What this band had to say was simply true, good, and right. This was the birth of my political convictions; they advocated direct action, animal rights, and environmentalism. From then on I collected all the material and information about anarchism I could get my hands on, often thanks to older friends.

In the following years I was a regular at the district library, where I made extended forays to track down everything that was related in any way to anarchism. Among other things, I dug out a few political science textbooks, in which there was shockingly little about anarchism. Nevertheless, I wrote out all the names that were mentioned in this context: Proudhon, Kropotkin, Bakunin, Malatesta, and all the rest of them. I recorded it all conscientiously. The specialized works on the topic were almost all in English and thus went over my head, as my language skills were only just sufficient enough to translate punk lyrics. Though *Anarchism—Practice and Theory* remained a closed book to me, at least I was able to locate an article here or there on Bakunin or Proudhon. The only book in Icelandic was a biography of Kropotkin, the author of *The Conquest of Bread* and a central anarchist thinker, a thick tome that I dragged home and plowed through from beginning to end. To my great disappointment, anarchism was barely even mentioned.

But I still had Crass. By this time I had also accumulated a remarkable archive of newspaper clippings, photocopies, and handwritten notes on which I kept what others had told me. One day I came across the magazine *Black Flag*, a British anarchist journal, which I used not only to improve my English, but also to establish contact by mail with anarchists abroad.

The more I learned about anarchism, the greater my certainty that I was an anarchist myself, and had always been one. Anarchy was and is for me the only way to a classless society, a mutually supportive society that respects the freedom of the individual and in which everyone can live his life freely and without external control, so long as he or she does not impinge on the freedom of others.

There was only one thing about anarchist ideology that I couldn't subscribe to at all, and that was violence. As a child, I myself suffered from domestic violence for years, in the form of psychological abuse from my father, and I would never agree to inflict it on others. Violence was and is the dark side of human coexistence. Anarchy and peace, that's what I longed for. This conviction led me to the teachings of Gandhi, and from Gandhi to Tolstoy and his Christian anarchy. Then followed a short detour through Max Stirner and his individualist anarchism, but in the long run I couldn't identify with it. The Christian anarchists were ultimately only a detour as well, since so far, despite repeated sincere attempts, I haven't managed to believe in a God.

Anarchism and surrealism are for me two sides of the same coin. I've read loads of stuff about these topics over the years and also had some personal experience of them, and both have shaped me and my perspective on life and our world decisively. In art, too, surrealism and absurdism have always fascinated me—in painting, film, and comedy. Surrealism, just like anarchism, means believing unconditionally in your dreams.

There are countless species and varieties of anarchism. Anarcho-syndicalism and anarcho-feminism in particular have left a powerful imprint on me. But there's a lot of truth in surrealism. We humans tend to want to explain, classify, and define everything. This is one of the benefits of our highly developed brains and is often used to divide the world into halves: wheat and chaff, right and wrong, black and white, positive and negative, beginning and end. Logical, binary thinking. For most people, reality is a fact. For the Surrealists, it's a dream.

As I said: An anarchist is someone who criticizes society from the comfort of his armchair. That's not entirely wrong. Anyway, eventually the rebellious anarchist Jón started a family, got himself a job, and rented an apartment. I hadn't graduated from school and so had only limited opportunities for work. Eventually, I began to try out comedy and acting, gradually got into the business, and eventually made it my profession.

BEING SILLY

As a small boy I wanted to be a circus clown. I dreamed of joining a circus troupe abroad and traveling the world. My parents and teachers were less enthusiastic about such ideas. In their view, having fun was something you kept to a minimum, not made a career out of. Comedy was at best the icing on the cake, but never the main thing in life.

My teacher said, "Jón, with all this silliness you'll never amount to anything." Since then, I've probably proved the contrary.

Without a robust sense of humor, I'd probably be in an asylum right now. Right from the start I had an insatiable appetite for any kind of comedy—on records, in television shows, and in films. In comedy I saw an opportunity, a future that no one else seemed to have noticed. I was crazy about *Fawlty Towers* and *Monty Python*, and saw every comedy I could catch at the cinema. When I was eight, I made my first joke. At school events, I was always the center of attention and seized on every opportunity to fool around. I loved puns, malapropisms, and corny witticisms. I ascertained very early on that I could go into a regular trance and really take off into flights of fancy. I was frequently told off for this by adults. It was as if they found this kind of thing unpleasant. Is happiness something embarrassing, something we should be ashamed of? Anyway, I was always being told to stop fooling around.

As I got older, I realized that if I was going to get into comedy, I first had to be an actor. But to get to drama school, I was reminded by my teachers, I'd need to graduate from high school. And as I thought it unlikely that I'd ever have enough staying power to get as far as my high school diploma, this dream too burst like a bubble. The alternatives looked depressing: I'd struggle through life on poorly paid jobs and do the Sideshow Bob bit at weekend parties. And so it proved. When I was eighteen, at one such party I met a guy in the same situation. He was gifted, imaginative, and original, he had impressive artistic abilities, but at school he stuck out like a sore thumb. His name was Sigurjón Kjartansson. Sigurjón was a founding member of the group HAM, with Óttarr Proppé (who was later elected to the city council, standing for the Best Party) and Sigurður Björn Blöndal (now my assistant and policy adviser).

Sigurjón and I liked chilling out together and cooking up mischief. Óskar Jónasson, a good friend of Sigurjón, had just started his studies as a film director and had already shot a few short films. When he was commissioned to make a TV comedy show, he brought in Sigurjón to play a small supporting role. Together we worked out a few sketches.

I had just taken the exam to be a cab driver and started a career working nights in Reykjavík. So comedy was just meant to be a nice little side job, a hobby, a source of relaxation in my leisure hours. But it suddenly developed its own momentum.

The year was 1993, and while I was gradually making a name for myself in comedy, Davíð Oddsson, then prime minister and a former mayor of Reykjavík, was chomping on his first Big Mac in the first McDonald's on Icelandic soil.

The live hijinx in which Sigurjón and I indulged had now done the rounds, and since good comedy was in short supply, we were invited to a gig at the summer festival of the Icelandic Toyota representatives. We were even paid for it. For the same money, I'd have had to drive my cab for a whole weekend. I soon realized that I could fill a gap in the Icelandic market with a new kind of comedy. The passengers in my cab patted me on the shoulder and said, "Keep it up!"

Thanks to the summer festival we had made a name for ourselves in certain circles, and it didn't take long before we were booked every weekend. We tried to build up the most versatile repertoire possible: a bit of stand-up, a few sketches, and musical spots in between. However, Sigurjón was also playing in his band, so it sometimes happened that he was double-booked. Then I had two choices—either kiss my act goodbye just because Sigurjón couldn't be there, or do the act without him and pocket the full fee alone. A no-brainer—apart from the fact that I didn't have the guts. Just the thought of standing alone onstage made me dizzy. The sketches we did together would have to be dropped completely, and the musical numbers too—I'm about as musical as a bottle of semi-skimmed milk—so stand-up was my only choice. Standing alone on stage and telling jokes.

At first I had a pretty bumpy ride. I was inexperienced and nervous, and response from the audience was limited. Some things worked, others just didn't. So I gradually threw out the bits that had flopped and focused on the successful numbers until I'd cobbled together a twenty-minute program. Suddenly people started listening—and started laughing. I even got used to heckling, and developed a special technique to counter it. The stage was no longer a place of horror, and in the meantime I was having a load of fun. My confidence was given an enormous boost, and suddenly I felt at home—which was in turn communicated to the audience.

I am convinced that humor will soon be recognized as a key skill for all areas of life. In my view, if you don't have a sense of humor, then you've got problems. It's a perfectly natural development. In the future it won't be enough that you're good at your job and get along with other people—you'll have to be entertaining too. But, like emotional intelligence and what is often derided as "feminine intuition," humor is still often viewed with skepticism, and the more screwed-up a society, the more likely it will develop such prejudices. All this will change in the future. If you can't raise a smile and never have a quip on your lips, you'll be viewed askance and, perhaps, ignored.

Only when humor has been universally recognized as a crucial character trait will the inhabitants of this world get along. They will realize that life is too short to get mad and fight among themselves; instead they will try to wrest as much pleasure and fulfillment from life as possible. Already the word *humor* itself is starting to appear with new meanings and in new contexts: a humorous government, humorous methods, humorous finances, humor during sex, humor in art and culture. Many people will dismiss these visions of a society based on laughter, comedy, and humor as childish and absurd. But I simply see it as the logical development of human thought. In other words, if you want to be one step ahead in the future, you're going to need humor.

THE FINANCIAL CRASH

With the privatization of the Icelandic banks, everything changed. What happened was not all that complicated. A handful of powerful financial moguls decided to make a present of the state-controlled banks to their rich pals—or to entrust them with the banks for a handful of loose change—in return for various favors. Suddenly the Icelandic banks, which had previously been a bit provincial and narrow-minded, seemed really cool.

And then everything went crazy. A new elite began to emerge, people who just juggled virtual money, drove Range Rovers, and spouted pseudo-business jargon over the phone. Within a few years, the banking sector had ballooned into a giant bubble, and finally the banks had accumulated loans and other assets totaling about ten times Iceland's GDP.

The politicians stood by and did nothing; they didn't understand this new world, and ordinary citizens started to smell a rat. The president assured us repeatedly that there was no cause for concern. It was just a load of cool guys, the Vikings of the modern era, sailing out into the world, robbing and plundering, and then returning to their home port with their ships filled to the brim with gold, women, and slaves.

Loans were easier to get than ever before. Banks threw their cheap deals around and any old Santa Claus could clomp into the next bank and take out a loan. If you wanted to buy a flat, you just signed on the dotted line and it was all yours. The slogan was: "Tell me what you want—and we'll lend you the money. That's our job." Ordinary people were only too happy to fall for the idea that those wily financial Vikings knew exactly what they were doing.

But eventually time was up and we had to face the bitter truth: it had all been done on credit. And then came the great reckoning.

In 2008, almost overnight, everything collapsed. The government convened an emergency meeting and mulled over the situation deep into the night. Outside, the journalists glued their noses to the windows and tried to find out what was up, but the politicians just said "no comment." The situation did however seem pretty serious. Then came the prime minister's speech. He stated that the Icelandic banks were virtually bankrupt, and if appropriate measures were not taken pronto, the country was threatened with national bankruptcy. He ended by heaving his now legendary sigh: "God bless Iceland."

Wherever two or three were gathered together, there was only one topic of conversation, and people outdid each other spinning the bleakest scenarios for the future. The unemployment rate would rise to 25 percent. A second crisis was already on the way. There were persistent and vociferous protests from citizens who assembled with pots, pans, and wooden spoons on the square in front of the Althingi, Iceland's national parliament, and organized one hell of a racket— the so-called "saucepan revolution"—whereupon, in January 2009, the government resolutely resigned.

I popped into town now and again to have a look at the spectacle, but didn't feel any need to mingle with the demonstrators. Waves of anger and aggression spread. Clashes with the police were reported almost every day, as when angry mobs broke into public buildings to disrupt streamed live sessions. Then parliamentary elections were called for April 2009 and a new government elected. It was the first purely left-wing government in the history of the Republic. Our expectations of the new rulers were high, but—not least because of the strict requirements of the International Monetary Fund, which had offered a financial package—their room for maneuvering was extremely limited.

Meanwhile Davíð Oddsson settled into the executive chair at the Icelandic Central Bank, and the protesting citizenry swiftly joined him there. The people demanded his immediate resignation—he was Davíð Oddsson, the human face of the crisis! I myself was well pleased to see that the ramshackle ruling party finally being dumped. Sjálfstæðisflokkurinn, the Independence Party, once a solid, dependable party that relied on common sense rather than lip service, had degenerated into a rotten, corrupt clique. Its ministers refused on principle to admit to their own mistakes, wriggled out of every tight squeeze, and flipped the bird to everyone else.

After prolonged civil protests and a legislative change by the Althingi, even Davíð Oddsson had to pack his bags. The Swedish daily *Dagens Nyheter* then named him as the "lousiest central bank governor of all time." In *Time* magazine, he was ranked among the twenty-five key people to blame for the international economic crisis. After his sacking from the central bank, Davíð moved seamlessly into the executive suite of *Morgunblaðið*—Iceland's oldest daily newspaper and loyal mouthpiece for the conservatives—whence he now regularly has his say in editorials and columns, detailing what a silly and completely incompetent mayor I am. To date, he has not admitted to a single mistake, let alone apologized to anyone, and he remains as convinced as ever that neither he nor his party bear any share of the blame for the economic misery.

Since then, many people have been racking their brains over what actually went wrong. How exactly did the financial crisis happen? When I look at the people involved in the banking collapse, all those officials, politicians, journalists, and business leaders, I wonder what they all have in common? They have different social backgrounds, different hobbies, and different lifestyles. Some are on the left, others on the right. At first glance it's impossible to make out any pattern. If there is one common denominator, however, it's the Icelandic universities. Those people were mostly educated in Icelandic universities and colleges. And strangely enough, many of those who sat in the control tower of the Icelandic economy before the crash have resurfaced as university lecturers again. Most of them come from backgrounds in the social sciences, and so have studied economics or business administration, law or political science—and practically nothing else. We call them experts. Before these people enrolled at university, they went to high school, where they were often already politically active in party youth organizations or a debating societies.

Representatives from the business and political worlds have come before the public and acknowledged their complicity in the banking crisis. However, I do not know of anyone in science and research apologizing for anything, or even noting that the universities had played a part—as the eggs from which the crisis was hatched, and the breeding grounds in which the financial Vikings were trained.

In some ways, the Icelandic educational system seems beyond criticism. Many people think it's close to perfect. It's not that I want to mark down our educational system as a completely useless and failed institution. But at school, creative thinking is not valued. Less than 10 percent of modules demand any degree of creativity. Most lessons are spent cramming students with knowledge that they have never specifically requested.

Yet this is what's being sold to them as a prerequisite for any success in life.

If we want a real democracy, we need to sow the seeds for it in our primary schools. In a truly democratically organized school system, parents and pupils could decide together what they want to learn. They'd at least have a certain say in the matter. In short, students need to be trained to be something more than experts. Yet we've never yet seen anything of the kind implemented anywhere. The only way to change the school system in the long term seems to me to start it all over from scratch and under different circumstances. Of course, it's doubtful that this is going to happen in any conceivable future.

THE THIRD WAY

In 2009, I worked in an advertising agency as a creative director. But in times of recession and far-reaching austerity measures, people everywhere were being sacked; others found themselves suffering from cuts to their salaries. Even in the television industry things were getting increasingly tight. So I left my job in an agreement with the agency and without much regret. My future was hazy, and I was in a state of total limbo. And it was precisely to get out of this haze that I made the decision to go into politics.

First of all, the financial crisis led to a rapid decline in purchasing power. Prices soared and wages plummeted. I had to service a loan from the year 2000 and was also paying off a car, with credit that I'd received in foreign currency. With the fall of the Icelandic króna these loans grew immeasurably, so the car was suddenly worth as much as a small apartment.

In those weeks and months, politics was virtually the only topic of conversation. The politicians had failed. They were idiots and assholes. Even though everyone was glad the Independents had finally been got rid of, the Left did not prove to be much better. So the elections hadn't changed much, just the faces in power. What was missing was something really new. Something different from our well-worn, dull-as-ditchwater party politics. What was missing were new words, new concepts, new values, and young, fresh faces. It was high time that the politicians left their hackneyed phrases behind and moved on from the rigid, outdated right-left pattern of thought.

So what do you do when you have to choose between two options, both of which are equally bad? You invent a third.

I'm often asked how I actually came to found the Best Party. The answer is that I simply came up with the idea. An idea is born when two other ideas have sex with each other, and a third comes into being. Though in this case we should perhaps describe it rather as group sex, as to begin with there were a whole bunch of ideas in play that eventually gave rise to this new one. Either way, once it was out in the world there was no turning back. It was just too brilliant.

Here's how it happened.

At that time, the International Monetary Fund held the financial reins in its hands, and industry insiders were sure that the first thing it would cut would be the cultural budget. All grants and scholarships for artists and creatives would be radically reduced, and there were even rumors of plans to close down the Icelandic State Theatre. Being a TV star or actor was not exactly a promising career in Iceland at this time.

Despite these circumstances, something new

opened up for me. A fellow director wanted to bring me in on a sketch show. I said yes, and we started talking over the new project. And that's where the idea for the Best Party first appeared. I had invented a character for this sketch show, a simple-minded local politician with an autocratic demeanor and completely absurd campaign promises. His motto and party logo was "Thumbs up!" He himself was an odd mixture of Groucho Marx, Tony Blair, and an American used car salesman. I experimented with sayings such as "Anything and everything for our underdogs!" or "All kinds of the best of everything!" and called the party for which he was a candidate *Besti flokkurinn*—The Best Party: "Why choose second best when you can have The Best?"

I invented other slogans of the same kind, the dumber and flatter, the better. At first we had a few other ideas on our list, but they got dropped pretty quickly. In between, I slipped into the role of the politician, intoned a few silly slogans and put on a stupid fixed grin. The idea never bore fruit, however, and with good reason. Once the protest demonstrations in front of the Althingi had become a daily ritual, we saw that it wasn't the time to palm this particular story off on a television station.

In those days we'd always be running into someone who'd lost his job or had to accept a salary cut. Most were burdened with foreign currency loans, which the free fall of the króna had blown into absurd sums. All these people woke up one fine morning to find that their debt had increased a hundredfold. The mood of anger and insecurity gave me and many others quite a few sleepless nights. How could it be that a whole class of society had kept a lookout for their own profit alone and persuaded the politicians to inflate that profit more and more? Up until then, in my view, all politicians were pretty much the same, a few alcoholics here and troublemakers there, like everywhere else, but by and large decent people, even if not the most stimulating of conversationalists. But that was obviously a huge misunderstanding.

Many of my friends and acquaintances regularly took part in the protest rallies. They met outside Parliament, whistling and roaring and rattling their cooking pots. A police security contingent had encircled the area and had to listen to the demonstrators' crude insults. I thought this was just incredible. What had the police done to these people? I remembered how many times my father had probably been involved in something similar. This kind of popular anger pissed me off. When the angry masses attacked Prime Minister Geir Haarde's car with fists and stones, while the prime minister crouched behind his car looking terrified, I felt really sorry for him.

I myself never took an active part in the protests. If I occasionally mingled with the demonstrators, it was less to make a statement than simply to be there. There was quite a special mood at the time, and quite a special rhythm. Then, one day, I had to watch as the furious masses invaded a café to disrupt the live recording of a New Year's Eve broadcast. At that moment, I'd finally had enough, and my attitude towards the saucepan revolution took a sudden turn. The journalists present were all more or less friends of mine, people with whom I'd worked for twenty years. When I saw their frightened eyes, the anger and rage inside of me grew. Suddenly, I just wanted to get away, away from this whole mess. I buried myself for hours and days on end in the Internet and tried to read up on the business and financial world. But the more I read, the less I understood.

In the advertising agency, I'd devised a complete corporate design for the Icelandic telecommunications giant Síminn. One of our biggest customers was the Kaupthing Bank, for which I had once written a commercial. At that time, the agency had even sent me to L.A. to do an interview with John Cleese of *Monty Python*, who was slated for the lead role. John Cleese was my childhood hero, but sitting opposite him, I realized that I too was basically nothing more than a cog in this giant machine. I worked for the advertising guys because they paid well. A commercial for Síminn was more expensive than a complete comedy series that I was filming. What the hell was actually going on in this country?

WHAT YOU NEED TO
BE A POLITICIAN

Do you have to understand something down to the last detail before you can contribute to it? Do you have to be a scientist to become interested in science? Do you have to know everything about nature to take pleasure in it? No. And it's no different with politics. You don't need to be a politician to have the right to participate in political life. You don't need special training or any special skills. You don't even need to be able to get on well with other people. Each of us has the right to become involved in politics just because we feel like it. If I book a trip to Rome, I don't have to know everything about the history of Italy or the culture of the ancient Romans. I can just go there to enjoy the beautiful weather.

I'm often asked whether being mayor is difficult. The question shows the kind of image we have of politics and politicians—and thus how easily we fall into a vicious circle: Politics is difficult and therefore only certain people can be politicians. People who can think fast and talk fast, people who are robust and can stand the heat. A bit like superheroes. The ideal politician has everything under control, is never at a loss for an answer, and shows foresight, determination, and know-how. No matter how much the media are sniffing around him, he always remains cool. There is nothing he doesn't know or understand, he never bursts into tears and never has any doubts. Unfortunately, he has hardly any human traits either.

Why have our politicians turned out like that? Who made them this way? The answer is: We did. All of us. We have neglected democracy, we haven't been paying attention and in some ways we've let ourselves get taken for a ride. Only a hair-thin line runs between the worlds of finance and politics. In the financial market, people are considered resources; in other words, the financial moguls have simply bought up the politicians. An investment like any other. Donors with money to burn invest in parties and politicians.

Experts and professionals are good and important, but they shouldn't be overestimated. We can't leave the schools to teachers, we can't leave science to scientists, and we can't leave democracy to politicians. We're so focused exclusively on success that we've forgotten how to enjoy things. And that's understandable. We live in an extremely success-oriented society. We want success in our professions, we want success for our children at school, and we want to learn about the successes of our government in the media. But success has its price. That price, in part, is joy in life. Because ultimate success does not exist. There's always a bit more to do. You need to go ever higher, faster, further, better. Success is easily addictive. As the saying goes: "For the alcoholic, one glass is too much and a hundred glasses are not enough." Man has flown to the moon— a decisive step, to be sure. But once he was up there, he made a disturbing discovery: there was nothing to do. That's why nobody's been back to the moon. Now they want to send a manned spacecraft to Mars, and there's nothing wrong with that either, as long as it's fun. As soon as something is no longer fun, it's worthless, pointless, and sick.

If someone gives you a brand new iPhone, you're happy of course, and that happiness lasts maybe a few days. But after a month, the phone is no longer quite so new, and eventually, when it breaks down, the happiness evaporates. But the person who gave you the iPhone is happy for maybe years to come. Because he's one of the good guys, and has given something. And that makes him proud and glad. The same is true for active participation in a democracy. It is high time that we get involved, not because we're obsessed with success—but because we want to have fun.

The political arena is a tough place. Success is based mainly on quick wit, charisma, and tricks. Rough-and-tumble is de rigueur on the political stage. On television we get to see the banter of parliamentarians every day, and we experience firsthand how they finish each other off. We see how a politician, even when he's just getting out of his car, is besieged by a horde of journalists and bombarded with questions—which he breathlessly answers. It's also a popular ploy, obviously, to trap the politician after a long and tiring session and to force him to give an interview.

What halfway sensible young man is so fascinated by the TV news that he thinks to himself, "Hey, great, I'd like to do something like that! I'll go into politics"? Surely very few. After all, most politicians don't cut a particularly sympathetic figure. Those who advocate a better society and want only the best for its citizens are just wimps. But should the slightest suspicion arise that they might have skeletons in their closet, people start pointing a finger of accusation. And not everyone is made to survive in such a world. This in turn has the consequence that when we hear the phrase "professional politician" these days, we usually imagine a skilled, well-trained expert.

Although this "profession" requires no special training, it does require special qualities. The professional politician is, as I said, a lightning-fast thinker with robust self-confidence and an answer to everything. Glimmers of humor can't hurt him so long as he uses them to pull one over on his opponents. In politics, a sharp wind blows, and only a few can stick it out. Here it's the typical male characteristics and values that are needed, which is why it's not surprising that female politicians often adopt a somewhat masculine persona.

If we want to change politics, we need to change

this entire frame of mind, to rethink what is really required to be a politician. To save democracy, politics must attract a wider range of people. We need scientists. We need artists. We need quite ordinary people who think slowly instead of quickly. People who admit it when they don't know something, instead of pretending they know everything so they won't be ousted from their jobs. We need shy people. We need the overweight, the stutterers, and the disabled. Punks, bakers, and manual workers. And above all, we need young people. We must make our politics more interesting, exciting, and cool, so that everyone will feel like getting involved.

After all, politicians are no different from the rest of the population. Strictly speaking, a politician is nothing more than a baker. There are good and less good bakers. Some are quite excellent bakers, others get nothing baked. The vast majority lie somewhere in between. Middling bakers, as it were.

In interviews I always arouse irritation when I openly admit that I don't know something. Or when I turn my interviewers' words against them. Sometimes I turn up at official occasions in drag or some such outfit. This too sometimes creates a bad impression, as it stirs up the suspicion that I lack seriousness. But it's just the opposite: I take my job very seriously, and am just trying to turn it into something a bit more entertaining. This is my way of standing up for the changes that I think necessary.

It's sometimes happened that a journalist inter-
viewing me has been left helpless with laughter at my
answers. In the TV news, that kind of thing obviously
gets cut. News is a deadly serious affair—a phenom-
enon, by the way, that's not limited to politics. News
programs are usually nothing more than a succession
of horrors. It often reminds me of a church service,
a deadly serious ceremony, which always follows the
same pattern.

OUR GOALS: A NEW KIND OF POLITICAL PROGRAM

Jón Gnarr wrote the party program to inaugurate the Best Party website in January 2010.

Our party program combines the highlights of all the other parties' programs. We rely primarily on concepts that have proven themselves in the welfare states of northern Europe. That sounds pretty good when you first hear it. Both the state-controlled planned economy with its paternalism, and the laissez-faire and market ethos of neoliberalism have failed, while societies that embody an active democracy seem to be quite resilient. In welfare states, social justice is much better developed than elsewhere, even with an extremely competitive job market. This is a good thing. We Icelanders have over the years moved increasingly away from the line followed by the Scandinavian welfare states and we must now pay the bitter price. The economic crisis has hit us particularly hard and meant the crash was deeper for us than it was for most of our neighbors. Unfortunately, the mood in the country is correspondingly lousy. That's why the Best Party now really has to roll up its sleeves and be a model of reconstruction, economic stability, social justice, and a better standard of living, a torchbearer to free us from the dark ages and lead us into a better future. We want to maintain freedom of trade and an open, non-state-controlled economic order.

To be honest: We don't have any party program of our own. But we still act as if we did.

The Best Party is a liberal, rock-solid party with a Scandinavian twist. We want to tackle the urgent problems that affect us all and set in motion far-reaching social reforms, operating with the necessary farsightedness and not neglecting social justice. We defend the systematic statehood and economic and cultural independence of Iceland, including its parliamentary democracy and its legal system. Citizens are being extremely cautious these days. That is understandable. For us, individual human beings are paramount, and by that we mean women as well as men. We don't think that women are naive fools who only come out with trivial crap, but serious people who have something to say: their voices must be heard. Therefore, we want to open a women's cafe, where women can indulge in every imaginable specialty coffee, in flavors such as vanilla or cinnamon, while chatting away to their hearts' content and slagging off whoever and whatever they want—and every word will be recorded and carefully archived. We'll also arrange mystery tours for our grandmothers and grandfathers.

As a transparent, democratic reform party we are

also planning to set up an Ideas Bank, a Sustainability Center as we shall call it, to provide citizens with a forum where they can present their ideas for the future and give them a transparent environment for discussion. The best ideas will be rewarded with a solemnly conferred special prize, also favoring sustainability. (For example, how about training the whales and fish off the Icelandic coasts?)

In addition, we are committed to environmental protection: we want systematic recycling, a transparent use of natural resources, electric cars, and less pollution of the air and the environment, all on the basis of equality and equal authority—in line with the values of our party. We do not smoke and we do not drink alcohol. We will turn up at all meetings and gatherings and, whenever possible, be in a good mood—we will also be thoughtful, take responsibility, and make decisions.

We want a new society—the best society that ever existed!

DEMOCRACY

Democracy is not perfect. It can be extremely tedious and time-consuming. Democracy stands or falls with participation and involvement. Democratically organized states don't have an easy go of it in times of crisis. It is still to this day the most equitable social order that man has invented. When Iceland was enjoying a turbo-capitalist boom, we put our democracy too thoughtlessly at risk. Now we have to pay for this.

Politicians in democratic states are a fairly uniform bunch; they can organize themselves into crossover associations that share a certain ideology and by which they are linked internationally. For example, the Swedish Social Democrats are pretty good buddies of Socialist Democrats in other countries, they meet at Social Democratic Party meetings and international congresses. The same is true for the Green Party or the Conservatives.

If we don't get involved, we neglect democracy, and it evolves accordingly. In one way, what prevails in the Western world is a kind of political inbreeding. True newcomers are extremely rare; after all, things are not made easy for them. A new arrival gets in the way and is therefore unattractive. In the few cases where a new arrival succeeds, such as the Pirate Party in Berlin, which fights for transparency in government and open telecommunications policy, or the Best Party in Reykjavík, new political actors immediately find themselves in the spotlight of world opinion. This is stressful and takes some getting used to.

Everyone knows the feeling that creeps over us just before elections, the sense that we really shouldn't go and vote. That in any case, there's nothing on the ballot to stand by or identify with. And so we just choose the lesser of two evils. That makes things awfully complicated. And behind it all, behind the politicians, political parties, and movements, stands the System, the apparatus that ultimately holds the reins in our society. And there again everything is based on rules and laws, but also on customs and traditions, and not infrequently on the views or personalities of individuals. In many democracies there is, besides the actual, official system, a second power structure that blossoms and flourishes in tandem with it—a System based on corruption, organized crime, opportunism, sleaze, and the black market.

Everyone wants freedom and direct democracy and individuals with the power to decide. But when it really comes down to it, only a tiny number want to make use of this power. Why? It's obvious—those who decide must also take responsibility themselves. Having power is always good, and freedom too, of course, but both are connected with responsibility. Without responsibility, freedom turns into chaos and power to dictatorship. Perhaps this is exactly the problem that the modern democracies face. Take responsibility? Who wants to do that? It puts us off. How often have we seen a politician being put through the mangle in a live interview or talk show, or seen how the slightest error earned him a place in the newspaper headlines! We expect politicians to be infallible and superhuman. In so doing, we deprive them of their humanity. When they make a slip of the tongue, we make fun of them. If they have personal problems in their marriage or with other people, this gets exploited mercilessly.

Change requires courage and initiative. Grassroots movements promise only limited success. The System does not sleep and now knows exactly how to cut off new political movements from below—well before they are developed. We are all familiar with images of angry crowds battling it out with cops in bitter street fighting. Such actions generally achieve nothing. A lot of effort to no great effect. What they do achieve is in convincing society, the politicians, and the System to set up more surveillance cameras, or send out more policemen with even better equipment and more weapons. The only realistic way to change things is direct participation in democracy. Direct involvement. If you find politics dumb and boring, and politicians too, then you just have to create your own party or platform. If you find the politics of the others dumb, it's up to you get in and make it better.

Are you mad at the politicians and the conditions prevailing in this country? Would you prefer to write something in a blog or organize a demo? Why not use your time and creativity to find out how you can actively participate in democracy? Found a party or run for office!

How do you do that? It's actually pretty simple—you need a little imagination and some courage, and the rest follows. But before you begin, you need to make a few principles clear: What bugs you? What's wrong? Where's the problem? You're committed to environmental protection, but there isn't a Green Party in your country? Then just found one. Or there *is* a Green Party, but it's not working effectively enough? Then become a member and lend a hand. But be prepared to invest a bit of time that you'll have to take from other activities. Be prepared to make certain sacrifices. Time that you would have otherwise devoted to your family, your friends, your hobbies, or your work.

In earlier days I'd sometimes ramble on about what it would be like to found a party and become minister of culture. I'd make sure I could have my own comedy show with the public broadcasters, then admit to corruption and resign from ministerial office—but continue with the TV show. Even with my friends I kept starting off on this track, over and over, until they said, "So why don't you do it, instead of just talking about it? Why don't you just found a party?" And so that's what I did. The craziest, wackiest party that ever saw the light of day. I posted it on Facebook and created a blog in which I circulated surrealist prose on social issues. One article attracted some attention, and so it happened that the media dropped by and asked me for interviews.

So I went to the tax office and entered the Best Party as a not-for-profit organization. That's how you apply to found a political party. The whole thing took about an hour and cost 5,000 krónur, or about 30 euros.

As the Best Party had only just seen the light of day, the media paid me a certain, slightly patronizing interest. At first I must have been a kind of comic relief for them. I tried to use this to draw attention to myself, pulling out of an interview, giving impossible replies, or coming out with totally absurd statements. The political conditions in the country were, as far as I could see, completely out of control. One scandal followed the next. Public funds were being squandered on poorly planned, dubious projects. Politicians vied with each other to keep the citizens happy and promised economic stability, reliability, and responsible use of taxpayers' money. One hundred percent transparency. Meanwhile, the financial system had long since swelled into a giant monster that grew bigger and rolled on relentlessly.

I won't deny that the prospect of a steady job with a fixed salary—instead of never-ending, poorly paid drudgery—has played no small role in my political commitment, but I hoped to kill two birds with one stone: to have a job, and to commit myself to a good cause at the same time. And I was sure I wouldn't be a worse mayor than my predecessors. Many assumed that this would mean I'd cross comedy off my list of activities. But I can't say this has happened. I'm as much a comedian as I ever was. That's what I am, it's part of my personality. Comedy is neither my hobby nor my day job—it's my life.

THE CAMPAIGN

Half a year before the elections for the city council on May 29, 2010, the first opinion polls were published. The Best Party got zero-point-something percent. The public TV station interviewed me, and I didn't make anything of it. I laughed and said that, after all, it was still just the beginning—the run-up to an epoch-making victory. At that time I was acting as court jester at Reykjavík City Theatre for a pittance and at the same time writing a play.

Some politician had uploaded a yawn-inducing, tedious monologue onto YouTube. I looked at it. The whole thing was incredibly bogus and embarrassing, so I decided to do something similar. As a backdrop I chose a theater poster that was stuck behind the desk where I worked—the announcement of an American stage comedy from the fifties. With the morose face of the female lead in the background, my confused election twaddle took on a downright surreal quality.

At about the same time I was the guest on a popular talk show. With my TV make-up on, I met a woman who greeted me kindly. I greeted her back.

"We'll be meeting on the campaign trail!" she exclaimed to me in a jocular tone of voice.

"Yes, we will," I replied. When she'd gone, I asked the make-up artist who she was. The lady was called Hanna Birna Kristjánsdóttir, the incumbent mayor of Reykjavík. I clearly didn't have much of a grasp on Icelandic politics.

Our campaign played out primarily on Facebook, YouTube, and Blogspot. I didn't put in an appearance on any of the official candidates' tours. I declared on my Facebook page that I did not intend to waste time on sterile let's-get-our-sleeves-rolled-up conferences. When I was interviewed on TV, I tried to provide a large dollop of complete nonsense. When it came to unemployment, I suggested opening a Disneyland in Reykjavík. After all, it would create a lot of new jobs, and there would definitely be plenty of people who'd be willing to get into Disney costumes and sell cheap trinkets for a few krónur. And we could attract the unemployed with special offers—free admission on Mondays, for example, plus a personal photo with Mickey Mouse!

My friend and collaborator Heiða Kristín Helgadóttir took care of all the practical and organizational questions of Party work. I would have an idea—and she'd already implemented it. My sons also energetically joined it. We decided to create a homepage with the name bestiflokkurinn.is, and to make it the ugliest website that a party had ever put on the Internet. "Thumbs up," the international symbol for friendship, approval, and recognition was to be our motto and trademark. On the logo, the thumb was deliberately made a tad too long, which gave the gesture a somewhat racy look.

We chose the ugliest typography and most hideous color combinations that we could find. We unabashedly pilfered stuff from the websites of other parties. We copied fragments of text from their respective election manifestos and mixed it all up (in the proper surrealistic manner) into a unique cocktail, completely meaningless but totally positive. Early in the spring we moved our campaign office to the center of Reykjavík. We designed and sold buttons, stickers, and T-shirts, and tried to attract external sponsors. But no one wanted to give us any money, so we were more or less on our own.

As the election approached, poll numbers for the Best Party climbed inexorably higher. It was obvious that this was largely due to votes from the left-wing electorate: their loss was our gain. And the left-wing intelligentsia woke up too, and the movers and shakers in that camp came after me guns blazing. So I was reproached with, among other things, having formerly been a member of the Independents and the Association of Icelandic Libertarians. They also mentioned that I wanted to legalize cannabis. Some went so far as to put me on the same level as Silvio Berlusconi. Others went even further and compared me to Hitler. I myself was mainly amused—all this, after all, just proved that people now saw us as a serious threat.

The Independence Party initially seemed happy about our success, because it was at the expense of the Left. Otherwise, they didn't appear all that worried; in any case they didn't think we'd ever get serious. But when the poll numbers left no doubt that the Best Party was nibbling away at the Independents' vote as well, they realized they couldn't just stand idly by. The party dominates the executive suites of all the major media companies, and from those quarters the cry started to echo ever more loudly: the country's problems weren't going to be solved by silly antics. I responded with even more silly antics. Every time another party made any election promises, we sat down together and discussed how we could top them. The Left-Green Alliance promised children and teens free access to swimming pools—our response was to offer free admission for ALL—with free towels INCLUDED!

On the whole, all the parties kept their language politically correct. As soon as there was talk of immigrants or women's equality, they all trotted out their standard formulations, and their waterproof, carefully rehearsed slogans. Meanwhile I took the liberty of saying that the Best Party would also do something for women and girls, and even for the elderly and disabled. For the underdogs, you see. On the subject of immigrants, I reminded them that the man who had brought the toilet to Icelanders had also been a foreigner. To begin with, nobody had taken him seriously—but it was unlikely that anyone now would be prepared to go without his invention. Then I suggested launching a major campaign to promote the immigration of Jews—they'd definitely help us float the economy again.

Furthermore, I wanted to have a woman with a foreign last name on our list of candidates. I remembered Elsa Yeoman, a woman I knew from my time in the advertising agency, where she'd been in charge of catering for the workforce. Elsa was a clever and open-minded person and immediately said yes. When I learned of her Jewish heritage, I missed no opportunity to present her proudly and brag a bit about her: "The Best Party is not only the first smoke-free party in Scandinavia, but also the only party in Iceland that's happy to have a Jewish woman among the top candidates."

At that time, parties often flaunted their election propaganda on the pages of newspapers. They outdid themselves with their full-page ads and resorted to completely shopworn clichés. The slogans were devised by advertising agencies and were modeled generally on any phrases that had proven successful in Denmark, the United States, or elsewhere, the usual blah-blah about home, garden, and family. Most people could no longer bear this stuff. The newspaper advertising we invested in appeared in the classified section of a greasy rag. We inserted the following: "The Best Party is looking for men and women who want to change things." We were almost overwhelmed by the number of replies.

THE BEST PARTY: WE ARE BETTER THAN ALL THE OTHERS

This party platform, by Jón Gnarr and other party members, was written in April 2010.

1) Protection and support for Icelandic households
Families are the core of our society and are our greatest asset. The state has a duty to meet the needs of households and to campaign for the protection of families in all circumstances. Because they deserve only the best.

2) Benefits for vulnerable members of society
These people need our help and support. That's why we offer free use of the city's buses and free entry to all swimming pools, because everyone, even the poor or otherwise disadvantaged, should have the opportunity to move in comfort through our city after a nice clean shower.

3) An end to corruption!
We promise to fight all kinds of corruption—by indulging in it publicly and in full view of everyone.

4) Create equal rights
We all deserve only the best, no matter who we are or

where we come from. We will ensure that everyone gets the best, and do our best for every individual. After all, we all play on the same team—the best!

5) More transparency!

We think it's important that politicians always put their cards on the table so that the citizens know what's going on. We promise to implement that concretely in our party as well.

6) Active Democracy

Democracy is great, and active democracy even better. Therefore, we are committed to it.

7) Debt relief for everyone!

On this point we will simply let the people decide—because the people themselves always know best what's good for them.

8) City buses: pupils, students, and the disadvantaged ride free!

We can promise more cost exemptions than any other party—because we won't actually try to keep our promises! So we could promise all kinds of things, no matter what, from free plane tickets for women to free cars for the rural population.

9) Free dental treatment for children and the disadvantaged
This is a service that, so far, doesn't exist—so we'll promise it along with the rest.

10) Free entrance to the swimming pool for all, free towels included!
Probably nobody can resist this offer—it's an election promise of which we are very proud.

11) The banking crash: those responsible are now being asked to pay.
We think this too is only right.

12) Absolute gender equality
We promise absolute equality, because that is the best for everyone.

13) We also take women and the elderly seriously
Women and the elderly are in fact rarely given a proper hearing. Everyone seems to agree that these people have nothing substantial to say. We will change that.

JOKE!

Four weeks before the election, the polls left no doubt: The Best Party was now the strongest political force in Reykjavík. After each new poll, we got together and held a war council. We finally had to put in an appearance on the campaign trail. Also, we needed to tone down our silliness and come up with something sensible to say. So in interviews I was now serious and prudent. We took turns appearing at the campaign events, and soon realized that we didn't necessarily have undecided voters in front of us on these occasions, but rather the members and supporters of the respective parties. The cheerleaders, so to speak. They looked like normal people who came because they took an ardent interest in these matters. But if any average normal citizen drifted in, it was guaranteed to be some old fogy or whiner. It was pure theater.

In addition, we were invited to club meetings and gatherings of large companies for Q&A sessions with the public. I answered all questions honestly and conscientiously, but also took the opportunity to switch to a more casual tone. My message was roughly: "I'm doing this because I feel like it. Because we enjoy it. But if you vote for us, we'll take it very seriously and see the thing through. Is that a deal? If that's not what you want, just vote for the same lot as last time, and I'll start looking for another job. No hard feelings!"

When it became clear that the Best Party was well on the way to evolving into a serious political body, I found myself giving constant interviews and expressing myself on boring and complex topics such as kindergartens, the Reykjavík domestic airport, and various financial matters. After all, the voters had a right to know what concrete plans the Best Party had for seniors, children, or this or that interest group. I thought this was more like a poorly disguised attempt to lull us to sleep with the greatest possible boredom.

I responded doughtily, but every answer threw up two new, even more complicated questions. Finally, I pulled the emergency brake and said that until further notice I wouldn't be making any additional comment in the Icelandic media. Now that the truth about the financial crisis had come to light, the whole quagmire of corruption, racketeering, and money-grabbing in which they'd all—political parties, business, and the media alike—been involved was exposed. As such, I decided that I would only be made available to foreign journalists.

In those weeks we were out on the road all day, from here to there and back again. Everywhere it was nonstop talking, and I often turned up at meetings totally unprepared and with no idea what was really going on. The rest of the time we hung out in our campaign headquarters, drank coffee, and discussed things.

From time to time my wife Jóga came along with a proposal that I meet this or that person. For example, we still needed someone in our ranks with legal expertise. Jóga suggested Haraldur Flosi Tryggvason, about whom I knew nothing except that he'd once played saxophone with the Jupiters. And now I knew he was also a lawyer. So I met with him and his wife over a cup of coffee and mentioned that we were still looking for a lawyer. At first he was skeptical, but his wife spoke to him and begged him to accept the offer. He mulled it over, took counsel with his father, and finally said yes. After the election, Haraldur Flosi was made chairman of the energy company Orkuveita Reykjavíkur. He would play a key role in the financial restructuring of that company.

It proved particularly difficult to get women to join the Best Party. I emailed a lot of my women friends and encouraged them to join us, but most remained dubious. Those who did finally decide to join mostly stayed discreetly in the background rather than muscling in on the front line. I would love to have seen a greater proportion of women among us. Politics has always been an almost exclusively male world, and it often strikes women as daunting and alien. Trying to persuade a woman to join the Best Party was a bit like trying to get a woman to run riot with the boys in the football stadium. Difficult and well-nigh impossible, but I wish it had been different during the election.

The last days before the election went by in a total

trance. I slept no more than two or three hours per night. We held endless meetings. The rest of the time I went on the Internet, and when I dozed off at my computer I immediately woke up with a start because I'd just dreamed that I urgently needed to update my Facebook status. In the meantime I was alternately in the grip of abysmal resignation and naked panic.

Gradually, the highest-ranking members of the Reykjavík city council had come knocking on our door wanting to talk to me and my party friends. All were educated and experienced politicians who had been on the council for years and years, some of them for over two decades. I had no idea what kind of people they were and what they did exactly. They said they wanted to address a few urban policy questions with us, something about budgetary and financial measures, schools and kindergartens. In fact, they wanted to sound me out, to get a feel of what could be expected if I actually ended up sitting in the mayor's chair. I promised that, if this happened, I would treat them with trust and respect. I would show full appreciation for their know-how and their professional experience and would expect the same from them in return.

At that moment it dawned on me what a damn complex business I had gotten myself into and how shockingly little I understood about the job. I'd concocted the whole thing out of pure fun. I wanted to pull a few stunts and meet a few cool people. But what I had set in motion here was definitely several sizes too big for me. I was getting in over my head. I barricaded myself behind my hand-knitted anarcho-surrealism. I turned up at TV interviews totally unprepared and in garish outfits and spouted garbage. What would I do to protect children and teenagers? What would be the main points of my cultural policy? Would it amount to merging kindergartens and primary schools or closing them? Would the daycare fees be raised? All questions that, to be honest, I'd never thought about.

And then came the inevitable: I was systematically grilled on a major live television interview. The moderator organized a veritable cross-examination and took me apart good and proper, while I felt my coolness gradually diminishing to zero. I sat there, facing my opponent, completely naked and defenseless. I blushed, stammered, and sweated, and then I heard an inner voice whispering to me: "Jón, what are you doing here? What the hell have you let yourself in for? What have you set in motion? Get yourself out of it, pronto. Otherwise it's going to be a mega-disaster for you, your family, and your whole life. Or are you going to spend the next four years hanging around on stupid talk shows while people slag you off for being such a miserable failure?"

After the interview I was completely floored. I felt like I'd been violated. There was a roaring in my ears, everything was spinning in front of my eyes, and my thoughts and feelings were running wild. Finally I took my wife into my confidence and told her I was on the verge of throwing in the towel. She said that whatever I decided, I could always count on her. "Just do what's right for you," she said.

This was my make or break moment. My night at Gethsemane. I could still jump ship from the political movement that I myself had set in motion. On the other hand, didn't I also have a responsibility towards all those I'd dragged along with me? I invited my Best Party friends Heiða and Óttarr to an extended crisis meeting. These two could see things with a precision that I had lost. Heiða in particular always saw everything in crystal clear terms. "You've succeeded," she told me, "in setting something up in politics—and that's what many have tried, but none have yet managed. The Best Party works, and it's going to change politics—and not just here in Iceland."

Of course that was a comforting thought, but also kind of creepy. Did I really feel like devoting myself exclusively to practical matters for the next four years and shelving the whole of my previous life? Did I really feel like spending my time in meetings about day care centers, short distance public transport, protection of minors, and budgets? Did I feel like throwing my weight around on behalf of the construction of the new regional hospital in Reykjavík? Or spending months boning up on the operation and management of the domestic airport? What I seemed to be up against were almost exclusively practical matters—and that's really not my type of thing! I think creatively. My mental process is tangled, erratic, and uncontrolled. Four years as mayor of Reykjavík would be something like four years in jail.

A big election meeting was scheduled for the next day at Reykjavík University. In the evening Jóga sent me to spend some time in the bathtub. I lay in the hot water and mulled things over until I had grasped the situation. Of course they all wanted me to continue and see the thing through, but surely everyone would understand if I dropped it all. Then I thought of the countless people who actually wanted to vote for me. Did I really want to disappoint them? Simply chicken out, call the whole thing off, just before the big finale?

And in that moment, there in the tub, the decision was made.

I'd leave it to chance.

I'd do it. I shared my decision with Jóga.

I then reported to Einar Örn and said I'd made a decision. I'd *withdraw* the candidacy of the Best Party, I told them, and inform the election body. I'd lost track of things and didn't trust myself to do this job. Einar showed understanding and seemed to respect my decision.

"Joke!" I said. "I was just a bit hung over, but now I feel like a new me. Like Felix from the ashes!"

"Now at least they'll all think you're a total idiot!"

That night I slept extremely well—like someone who knows that he's made the right decision. The next day I told no one about it, not even Heiða. I put on a serious and troubled demeanor, quite contrary to my habit. The representatives of the other parties gave their election speeches. Then it was my turn. "At first I thought the idea pretty awesome," I began. "But then things got more confusing, and now the whole thing is kind of out of control. I'm not a politician. I am a comedian, and politics isn't my profession. Therefore, I hereby announce that the Best Party has decided to withdraw its candidacy from the upcoming city election."

There was silence. On the faces of the students, disappointment spread. The other candidates exchanged meaningful glances and concealed their satisfaction with difficulty.

"Joke!"

Then laughter broke out.

I explained in several ensuing interviews that it was high time that artists in Reykjavík took over the helm. Very few people were of the opinion that artists had any place at all in politics. But I hastened to point out to them that Iceland was known around the world for its art. It was our writers and artists in particular who ensured we had fame and reputation abroad, so it was high time to let Icelandic artists finally get the recognition they deserved.

AFTER THE ELECTION

The result was unambiguous. In the 2010 city council elections, the Best Party won 34.7 percent of the vote. The Independence Party, the old established Right, got 33.6 percent, the social democratic Samfylkingin 19.1 percent, and the Left-Green Alliance 7.1 percent.

The rest had fallen at the 5 percent hurdle.

I broke out in a sweat.

Later that evening, at our victory party, we sat around a kitchen table and discussed the results. The air crackled with tension, and we giggled nervously. What were the other parties going to do now? Would the Social Democrats team up with the Independents to form a working majority (and ignore the fact that this coalition had been in power in 2008 and was thus jointly responsible for the crisis)? Would their common aversion to us be a sufficient basis for political cooperation? What kind of a party were we after all? Who would we want to work together with? Not with those on the Right, we were unanimous about that. Of all the parties they were the rottenest. But what annoyed us even more was that they obviously had no respect for us. Whenever we had to deal with them, they made us feel their contempt and condescension. That said, I did think briefly about what it would be like to form a coalition with them:

"This party chairman, Hanna Birna, she's all right apparently, okay?" I said, thinking aloud. "What do you think?"

"Well, she's not exactly evil, but she is extremely superficial," someone said. "You know the interview in which she explains why the majority has fallen for her party?"

No, I hadn't come across it.

"She more or less says, 'What a pity, it would have been so easy to find a consensus.' Meaning, of course: if everyone else had done what *she* wanted. And I also very much doubt that Hanna Birna would ever voluntarily relinquish the mayor's office for you. You can forget all about that."

"But do I have any other choice—apart from becoming mayor, I mean? Isn't that what people want?"

"Yes, that's exactly what people want. The people voted for us because they want Jón Gnarr as mayor."

"So the Independents are out of the picture right from the start?"

Heiða nodded. "They think you're a total idiot. And we're not working with people who look down on us."

"Look down?"

"Yes. You know what they call you inside the party, right?"

I'd never given the matter any thought.

"They call you 'the Clown.' "

"Aha. And what about the Social Democrats? This Dagur Eggertsson? I don't know what to think of him, either. But I don't know him. Is he okay?"

Óttarr knew Dagur a bit better. "Dagur's a great guy," he said.

"But isn't he a bit . . . well . . . strange?" I asked. "For me, he was always one of those politicians who I can never make out. He speaks without commas, as if trying to set a world record, and it's as clear as mud to me. He just doesn't listen."

"Dagur definitely has his strengths and weaknesses," someone said. "But overall, the Social Democrats have a lot of capable people. Of course they also have cross-links to the leftist intellectuals."

"But by and large they respect us, I mean, more than the others, anyway."

"Yes, yes," someone said. "But only because they're afraid of us. We draw the most votes away from them. They're trembling with respect, so to speak."

General laughter.

"At least they seem to be not quite as puffed-up as the rest," someone said. "After all, they've already tried to contact us."

"And they could come to terms with me as mayor if the circumstances were right?" I asked.

"We still need to find that out."

"Okay, and how do you do that? Should I perhaps

call Dagur? Heiða, you're our political expert, you know about this kind of stuff."

"No," Heiða said. "Let's keep playing it nice and cool. Now it's the big guessing game, who's getting it together with who, and so on—and the media are guaranteed to get involved big time."

"It's a surreal situation, of course," Björn pointed out. "There's never been anything like this before. Not here in Iceland, and as far as I know nowhere else in the world."

"It's logical enough," I said. "Until now, there wasn't any Best Party either. Maybe a Most Acceptable Party, or an It'll-Have-To-Do Party." Laughter. "So, how do we proceed?"

"You stay in the background and keep schtum. You don't make any statements, not when any people from the press call, and not on Facebook either."

"But I could at least post that I *won't* be commenting in the Icelandic media, because they're all just willing henchmen of the whole political clique?"

Heiða and Björn shook their heads. "No, just don't. We shouldn't rouse the others against us more than necessary. They're all pretty much against us already so we don't need to provoke them any further. You just don't reply."

Then we decided that Óttarr and Sjón would represent the party in the coalition negotiations.

"And if the Independents get together with the Social Democrats?" I interrupted. "After all, there's something of a political emergency on. And we know what their club is like. If it comes to the crunch, they'll pull themselves together and wriggle out somehow."

"They won't risk it," Sjón remarked.

On the following days, exploratory talks were scheduled. Heiða, Björn, Óttarr, and Sjón met successively with representatives of the other parties. Otherwise, we sat around in the home of one of our members, drank coffee, and talked shop. The Leftists could obviously contemplate a coalition with us, and the Independents had already come knocking. They suddenly started behaving as if they thought we were an amazingly smart and alert bunch. We found this incredibly funny.

"Sjón and Óttarr had a conversation with Dagur earlier today," Heiða announced.

"Has he seen *The Wire*?" I asked.

"We did briefly mention it," Óttarr said. "No, he's never seen it. And he wanted to know if we would make that a precondition for cooperation."

"He must watch *The Wire*," I insisted. "What am I supposed to talk to him about otherwise—socialism?"

Gradually things took shape. The first meeting with the Social Democrats took place in an old factory building down at the harbor. For Samfylkingin, labor and education policy were top priority issues. We wanted most of all to make Reykjavík more human, more welcoming, and more modern. I want Reykjavík to be the hippest, coolest city in the world, and it must have more trees. In terms of citizen welfare and social security, we were largely in line. We wanted to advocate a minimum social standard, a statutory basic protection for the homeless and socially disadvantaged. In general, it was high time we paid more attention to the outsiders and disadvantaged. Too little is still being done for the underdogs at the bottom of the social ladder. I was one of those all my life.

The media indulged in avid speculation as to how things would pan out. But we kept quiet. In the roundtable discussions, the political experts provided in-depth analyses, declared the election of the Best Party to be a grotesque mistake, and said that I had no chance as mayor anyway. When the result of the negotiations finally became clear, I met Dagur for the first time in person. It was obvious that he would be taking a big risk if he formed a coalition with the Best Party. To some of his colleagues, this bordered on political suicide. That's why I decided to pay special attention to honesty and transparency in this conversation. I simply put my cards on the table.

"I want to do this job really well," I said. "I want to achieve something that benefits the city and its residents. Believe me, it's perfectly clear what's in store for us. But I guarantee I won't just drop everything and jump ship. Because I believe that, together, we can get some pretty cool stuff up and running. Still, I'd like you to be familiar with *The Wire*."

"No problem," Dagur said. "Where can I find this series?"

"I guess it's out on DVD by now. Or on iTunes. Oh, and I'll be mayor. That okay with you?"

"Sure."

A press conference was scheduled to announce that the formation of a coalition was now complete. But where would this press conference be held? The council usually gave press conferences in the Nordic House. Dagur suggested moving the meeting to Breiðholt, a densely populated, low-wage problem area of Reykjavík with a big immigrant population. I thought that was pretty cool. The Breiðholt Coalition.

"My brother lives there, in the largest residential block in the whole district," I said. "If I'm not mistaken, he's actually the janitor. How would it be if we held the meeting with him on the roof?"

I called my brother.

"Hello. Can we hold a press conference on the roof at your place?"

"Sure thing. Shouldn't be a problem."

"Do we need approval or anything?"

"No idea."

"Aren't you the janitor on the block?"

He wasn't the janitor. But he did have the key to the attic, so that was sorted.

At the press conference we announced the outcome of our discussions. I'd become mayor of Reykjavík, and Heiða would be my closest colleague and political consultant.

"And how will you tackle the job of being mayor?" the journalists wanted to know.

"I'm going to try and get my stuff set out neatly, and otherwise just be nice."

"Do you really think you can cope with the job?"

"Being mayor? Yes, I can cope. It can't be all that hard. It's a pretty relaxed job where you comfortably sit at a desk most of the time, isn't it? I've done all sorts of lousy dirty jobs in my time. I'm really not spoiled. I was a taxi driver in Reykjavík and actually got lost downtown. Didn't know any of the street names. But I got down to it. Brooded over the map and learned everything by heart, and eventually I was a really good taxi driver. And always polite, too. I held the car door open for ladies, and none of my passengers ever complained about me."

"What's the first thing you'll tackle?"

"I'm going to make sure that Reykjavík is hip and cool."

"And what is hip and cool?"

"Er . . . roughly the opposite of stupid and narrow-minded."

"And that request for a polar bear for the zoo?"

"First we have to make it council policy that no more polar bears get shot."

OUR MORAL CODE

Jón Gnarr described the self-image of the Best Party on the party's website in January 2010.

The following "rules of moral behavior" apply to city officials and fellow workers in the Best Party, as well as all those who represent us in committees and panels. They also apply to individuals who represent the party in public, in the media, on the Internet, or using other, similar technologies, including those that have yet to be invented. With their signatures, all party members agree to these rules and are committed to them. Any violator of the rules incurs criminal penalties and will be prosecuted. Only in this way can the conscientious observance of the rules be achieved.

Anyone who is suspected of violating the rules must temporarily relinquish office while relevant officials investigate the matter. If the suspicion is confirmed, the person in question will immediately be suspended from party membership and must surrender his or her party card as well as all articles that bear the logo of the Best Party, such as T-shirts, buttons, and pens. Also, all relevant information, photos, and text materials will be deleted from the archives of the Best Party.

Finally, the expelled member must make a personal apology by asking for the forgiveness of party members in writing, thus showing remorse and expressing the desire for reparation. This apology should include an expression of regret at causing damage to our party and its image, as well as the hope that the voters will not condemn the party as a whole, but recognize the violation as the mistake of one individual. Finally, the document is to end with some warm words about the party and its wonderful members, and then be published in easily accessible places in the main analog and digital media.

The rules in detail:

1) **Independence.** We are autonomous and independent and do not take any sponsorship money either from wealthy individuals or from large companies. If anyone should contact us with that intention in mind and offer us financial support, our answer in each case must be: *The acceptance of sponsorship from commercial companies violates Article 1 in our moral code!* However, it is not excluded that we may declare this point to be void where necessary, or at least rethink it and change its wording.

2) **Honesty.** We expressly decline to tell a lie. Should this nevertheless occur, we will admit it without

hesitation. If we are caught telling a lie, we ask for forgiveness and promise never to do it again.

3) **Personal hygiene.** We are always freshly washed and properly dressed. When we shower or bathe, we follow the guidelines of the Reykjavík Municipal Swimming Pool Company and clean our feet, armpits, and genitals in particular with the greatest care.

4) **Helpfulness.** Helpfulness is the actual core of these rules. We see ourselves as providing a service and are always willing to help—and this is part of the image of our party. When, for example, we come across some old granny who can't get by on her own, we are ready to help straightaway. We do not fail to ask a friend to record our helpfulness in a photo, which we can then later publish in the media or online.

5) **Cover-ups.** Keeping silent and covering things up are the archenemies of democracy. Therefore, we make no use of these practices, at most exceptionally and then only in self-defense. With us, everything gets said—except when it damages the reputation of the party.

6) **Confidentiality.** We treat everything that is said and done within the party in strict confidence and broadcast none of it outside—unless it is irresistibly funny, or especially beneficial to the reputation of the party and its leader.

7) **Good mood.** We are always happy and cheerful

and always have a smile on our lips. We endeavor to spread a good mood and not to show our inner selves to the outside world. Always remember that we are the best! If others are listening in, we become particularly lively in our discussions of our party, its image, and how much fun we are having. And we try to prove the point as convincingly as possible by laughing.

8) **Respect.** We show everyone respect. If we have no respect for someone, then we act as if we did. If someone tells us that we suck, we assure him what a great guy he is. We do not discriminate against anyone, not even the dumbest moron. We allow ourselves to disrespect people only when we are talking *about* them, not *with* them. This alone is the ultimate proof of true respect.

9) **Honesty.** We also always treat others sincerely and honestly, and expect the same from them. We never lie—unless we find ourselves forced to do so.

10) **Cooperation.** With us, everyone supports everyone else. We are a unit, not a random collection. If one of us publicly comes out with some piece of nonsense, we are loyal and say we share his opinion, even if that's not true. In this way we strengthen cohesion and team spirit within the party—and thus our image and popularity.

BECOMING MAYOR

I had no idea what a mayor actually did. We'd had mayors who were mentally unstable and others who were alcoholics. I was neither. What would an average working day look like? I'd probably be in my office sitting at my desk, signing a few documents and making a lot of calls. Then a debate about something or other, and then a concert or theater premiere. It didn't sound bad. And I would get a chauffeur—much to my amusement.

"What kind of car does he drive?"

"A Skoda Octavia."

"How respectable. Anyway, we can change that. We could buy an Explorer with tinted windows instead."

The next morning the driver picked me up from home. I was nervous, excited, and bleary-eyed. I'd lain awake all night. On the way to City Hall we stopped off at Heiða's, as she was going to be at my side as personal advisor for the first few months. When she was later promoted to the party presidency, S. Björn Blöndal took over, and he's done a good job as my assistant and advisor ever since.

City Hall had inspired some unease in me ever

since it was built. I had entered it only in exceptional cases, for example when one of the children had to go to the bathroom urgently, and I'd seen the building as cold and depressing every time. In addition, it stood for all the endless debates and countless scandals that had marked city politics in Reykjavík over the years.

We rolled into the underground car park beneath City Hall and parked under a sign that said MAYOR. From there we took the elevator to the third floor. The staff greeted me and introduced themselves. Deputy Mayor, Head of Department, Chief Secretary, Head Porter. I had no idea who was responsible for what. The office manager was Regína, a red-haired, feisty woman my age. I liked her immediately. She was quick-witted and seemed to have a sense of humor.

Then they presented me with my office, which more precisely consisted of two huge rooms along with a private bathroom, shower, and view of the Reykjavík city lake. Outside along the glazed front ran a balcony that looked out directly onto the surface of the water. On the desk gleamed a brand new MacBook Pro with a fifteen-inch monitor. My computer. Originally, they'd wanted to get me a ThinkPad, but I'd told them I absolutely couldn't cope with Windows.

Then Regína took me in detail through my rights and obligations. By now I'd realized that I had not only one new job, but several. I was the chief supervisor of the largest employer in Iceland. I had eight thousand people under me. Also, I was, politically speaking, the representative of the city council—and of all the inhabitants of Reykjavík.

Fuck.

Finally, the conversation turned to my family.

"And your wife will always be by your side?"

"Hm. I haven't thought about that yet."

"In general, the mayors decide for themselves whether and to what extent their spouse is a public presence."

Without my wife, nothing works for me. Our relationship is extremely close, and we try as much as possible to participate in each other's lives.

"I'd like her to be there, as often as possible in any case," I said. "So long as, well, it isn't too stupid or annoying for her."

"Would she go with you to premieres, openings, and similar events?"

"Absolutely. Even if we're not always the biggest of premiere goers. I just don't want it to turn into a form of torture for her."

"In two weeks the 'Forum of Scandinavian Capitals' is taking place in Stockholm. It will be a chance for you to get to know the mayors of Helsinki, Stockholm, Oslo, and Copenhagen."

Fuck.

"We have to organize the trip and book the flight. So will you wife be going too?"

"Er, that would be great, yes. Would she have to pay for herself?"

"No. You're entitled at any time to take your wife," said Regína. Then she added, "But you have to expect that the media won't leave it without comment."

"You mean that if my wife comes too, then the next day her photo may be all over the front page of *Morgunblaðið*, along with a headline along the lines of *Reykjavík's New First Lady: City Foots Bill For Luxury Trip?*"

Regína nodded. "Something like that. They're always phoning here. They'll jump on you and ruthlessly use whatever they can find."

"Okay. If so, I don't want my wife or my family to be exposed. I'll see it all through on my own."

"That will probably be best under the circumstances, I'm afraid," she agreed. "Unfortunately." There followed a long silence.

"Do I actually get any leave?"

"Yes, you have the right to four weeks of vacation per year, but you should, if possible, never take more than one or two weeks off at a time. Most mayors take two weeks over Christmas and New Year, and then two weeks in the summer."

"Okay."

"Now, in the first week you don't yet have a full schedule. It's a matter of you meeting people and making yourself familiar with how it all works here. I've made you appointments with all the major heads of department who'll give you the info on the different areas. Oh, and the city treasurer would like to have a chat with you and the Coalition soon, on the Orkuveita situation."

I attended the strangest meetings and gatherings. Quite early on, I took part in a video conference of the "Fund for West Scandinavian Cooperation," a cooperative project between the capital cities of Reykjavík, Nuuk, and Tórshavn to promote the goal of cultural exchange between these cities. So I sat in City Hall in front of a webcam, while behind me images of city council meetings in Greenland and the Faroe Islands were projected onto a screen. The wifi was quite weak, and as soon as someone moved too fast either the picture froze, or there was no picture at all. When I looked into the camera, I couldn't see the others. The sound came over the in-house speaker system, which, with the unstable online link, led to people sounding as if they had a wet dishcloth in their mouths. Since, to crown it all, I'm hard of hearing, I had great difficulty in following the discussion, especially since it was taking place in Danish, a language in which I had never excelled.

The whole thing was incredibly embarrassing, and at the same time rather comical. Luckily, we'd gone over the proposals before and had marked everything we wanted to approve. So Heiða stood on a chair, pressed her ear to the speaker, and gave a thumbs-up or down. Then I looked into the camera again and said either "Reykjavík siger ja" or "Reykjavík siger nej."

A CLOWN IN CITY HALL

After the initial hysteria had subsided and the voices of the critics and carpers gradually faded, people took a closer look and realized that many initiatives supported by the Best Party were correct and necessary. The merger of schools was well received on the whole. We merged the preschools into fewer and bigger units and also merged the primary schools with the after-school daycare centers. Students and parents were satisfied, and instead of skepticism and contempt we earned confidence and respect. Within the party, we tried especially hard to adopt a decent tone. We supported each other in our respective roles and took the time to talk about problems and to explain why we were doing or not doing this or that.

Soon, by a majority decision, I was appointed as the group's "Smokescreen." This meant I had the task of embarking on deliberate maneuvers to draw the attention of our opponents to me as a kind of decoy, a lightning rod for attacks and nastiness of any kind, so that others could focus on the party agenda. After all, I was used to attacks. And besides, it meant I could justify my nickname "The Clown at City Hall." So, for example, in a live interview I cheerfully admitted that there was plenty I didn't understand and certain questions to which I simply had no answer. This might have seemed like a distraction, but it was a plan to get back to work.

I've had all sorts of lousy jobs over the years. As an unskilled laborer on construction sites and in factories. As a taxi driver, psychiatric nurse, and caregiver in facilities for the disabled. For me there are no good and bad jobs. At best, a job can be done well or badly. So far, I've tried in every job to do my best, whether it was laying paving stones or packing plastic bags. If people are still not happy, there's almost nothing I can do about it. They just have to make do with me—or find someone else.

In the first one hundred days of my time in office, the media more or less left us in peace, only to pounce on us all the more mercilessly shortly thereafter. Newspapers published countless reports and articles about all my screw-ups and everything that was wrong about the city. Our political opponents couldn't get over my appearance, my fashion style, and God knows what else. Almost daily, journalists would call, on the hunt for new details about me and my work. The press were watching me everywhere, trying to make me feel uncomfortable and laying the blame for everything they could at my door. They used quotes from interviews I'd given, taken completely out of context, to prove what a failure I was. When we had a particularly snowy winter in Reykjavík, this of course was also my fault.

I did my best to react with calmness, patience,

and restraint. The fact that journalists didn't exactly love me came as no surprise; after all, I'd never spared them either, often throwing their own questions back at them or giving them incoherent answers. But the press obviously considered it their democratic duty to expose me. I had done my bit to encourage them with sayings like "The media are part of the problem, not the solution." But while they tried to wear me down, to general sympathy, my colleagues could calmly get on with work for the party. Most of them were quiet, restrained people from other professions, completely unaffected by the hurly-burly of the media.

In contrast, I grew up in an environment where violence and aggression were always on the agenda. Even as a stand-up comedian, I had been exposed to constant threats and harassment. Early in my career I didn't make much of a good impression; people were outraged and dismayed, some were even offended. I was accused of homophobia, racism, misogyny, and disrespect for central social values. I picked up no fewer than fifteen criminal charges for things that people didn't find funny. Plus a charge for attempted treason and criminal proceedings for trespassing in the Althingi.

Interestingly, among my aggressors I attracted the mentally disturbed in particular. For a while I was pursued by a woman who thought I would steal the thoughts of her sleeping children. Once, on the way home from my job at the radio station, a mentally disturbed man came at me with a sledgehammer. I ran and hid in a supermarket. Eventually the police came and pulled the man out of traffic. When the incident was reported in the media, the undertone of schadenfreude was unmistakable: finally, someone who was always dragging others through the mud had gotten his comeuppance.

Anyone who has ever tried to make comedy knows that he is thereby embarking on a fight against rejection, bigotry, and misanthropy. How many times have I stood on a stage in some low dive in front of a more or less drunk audience and had to listen to threats, verbal abuse, and humiliation. All this is to say that the sharp wind that was now whistling against me in the political scene was nothing new, and I defended myself by being provocative and even raising the wind myself. Sideswipes from the opposing camp left me relatively unfazed—the meaner and nastier they were, the better. As long as they worked off their negative energy on me, at least the others were spared such attacks.

From the beginning I tried to build up a good relationship with my employees, my colleagues, and the management team in the city administration. The city of Reykjavík is fortunate to have well-trained professionals with years of experience at its disposal. I treated each of them with respect, but also wanted to be respected in return. Very soon they all realized that I intended to go about my job seriously and sincerely, and wasn't just the unpredictable, crazy clown that many people took me for.

WU WEI

If there's one thing that has particularly influenced my fight against violence and negative energy, it's so-called sustainable transparency. Sustainable transparency uses the approaches and methods of judo and transfers them to interpersonal skills. In short, it consists of this: Instead of fighting negative energies, you simply let them sweep over you. You don't put up any resistance, but either give way or try to adopt the destructive power of your attackers and turn it against them. In Chinese philosophy, this principle is called Wu Wei, which literally means "let it happen" or "non-intervention."

I've read all the most important scriptures of Taoism and have trained in judo for years. It was always my greatest ambition in so doing to learn how to suggest to the enemy that he is unsure or afraid. I learned the various holds and throws, and how to make the other fall into a trap by pretending you have a weak spot. In other words, you lead your enemies to underestimate you, and as soon as they to seize the opportunity and launch an attack, the trap snaps shut—and they've lost. What most amazed me in judo was how blind to these strategies other people were. How they fell for the same trick again and again. It worked best with rough, primitive thugs. The coarser and more aggressive they were, the more easily they could be distracted and flattened. With them I just needed to pretend I was wiping the sweat off my brow, and already they felt safe and inattentive, just as I intended: I quickly responded—and that was that. In this way I defeated opponents who were twice as strong as me.

The point is to wear down opponents gradually, until they finally give up. In addition, this principle prevents you from stooping to the level of the attacker. Through this deliberate non-intervention you get the others to lose their balance. When, for example, someone gets terribly upset in a meeting and starts being noisy—the first level of violence—I just look into the face of the person concerned with big eyes and a simple smile. This in turn makes him even more upset. So he gets even louder and hurls empty insults around, because the absence of any reaction on my part makes him incandescent with rage. A surprisingly large number of people freak out at the slightest opportunity and don't pull themselves together until everyone is staring at them in perplexed silence. By that time they have not only lost their self-control, but also their dignity.

Here is one highly illuminating example of the Wu Wei principle: I was at a city council meeting, and as so often happens, the entire opposition took the floor, one after the other, to say what an idiot I was, that we were doing everything wrong, and how much bullshit we were coming out with. As usual, I was listening quietly, with a silly grin, as if I hadn't even grasped that they were laying into me. This led one of the city councilors to get so hot under the collar that he exploded. He let fly a volume of invective such as I have rarely experienced. I was lying, he spluttered, I was a retard and altogether not quite sane. I felt the anger slowly rising in me and shaping itself in my head into a few phrases that I'd have liked to hurl back at him: disgusting, mindless populist, mendacious, opportunistic ass-kisser!

But I bit my tongue, kept silent, and put on an even sillier grin. When the man had finished, he stepped down from the rostrum, shaking at the knees. The other councilors pulled dismayed faces and seemed edgy, some downright shocked. Their colleague had really gone too far with his personal insults and tasteless jabs. With a smile, I looked across at the chairman, put my hand up and asked to be heard. Although I was inwardly seething, although lies and baseless slander had just been uttered about me, I remained outwardly completely calm. And then I simply made his hate-filled tirade into the subject of discussion.

It was a pity, I said, that he had such a bad opinion of me. But unfortunately I was unable to concur with his view that I was an incompetent mayor. Because I considered myself to be really a pretty good mayor, although this was, of course, a relative matter. After all, this question, the question of good and bad, was one that the philosophers of antiquity had been chewing over forever, and we were hardly going to solve the problem just like that. Then I explained why I thought I was a good mayor, and ended by saying: "I want you to know that your impression of me is not reciprocated. I think you're on the level and I know that you're a great guy in many respects."

In the party, we've always placed this principle at the top of our agenda and always tried to base our contact with others on it: We return good for good, respect for respect, and friendship for friendship. We meet insults with courtesy, ill will with indulgence, and stubbornness with tolerance. In this way the good is always getting stronger. We have been criticized many times, in fact, for not putting up a decent fight. Truth be told, we've often let opportunities to get back at our opponents just slip away. Sure, the temptation is great, but if we yielded to it, we'd be no further advanced. Then judo is no longer judo, but a boxing match—and anyone who knows anything at all about those things knows that there is a world of difference between them.

MY FAMILY

My career as an actor and stand-up comedian has decisively altered the lives of my children. I have five children, and the age range between the oldest and the youngest is twenty years. Again and again they have been asked if their father was perhaps crazy; alternately, they have been congratulated and assured they could consider themselves lucky to have such a father. The talk show hosts and gossip journalists all want to come to my house to see me in my private life and include my family in an interview. That's why I decided very early on to draw a clear dividing line between the media and my family, and avoid dragging my wife and children into the spotlight.

But I try as much as possible to have a normal, healthy family life, and aim to provide a safe home and a good education for my children. In private, I make jokes rather rarely. At home, I'm more of a nerd.

The most important person on earth is and will remain my wife, Jóga, full name Jóhanna Jóhannsdóttir. We are an inseparable unit. Although we are two different individuals, we work and function as one. I never decide anything without discussing it beforehand with my wife. In return, she benefits from my judgment. I would argue that she made a much more decisive and energetic contribution to founding and organizing the Best Party than I ever could have. She always sees an opportunity where others see a black hole, and now our brains are so perfectly matched that they function together as a kind of super brain. I'm the principal actor, and she directs.

If I'm an exhibitionist, then my wife is the exact opposite. She hates any kind of spotlight or media attention. We appear as little as possible at premieres or openings and are extremely cautious when the press tries to rummage around in our private lives. My wife is a massage therapist, and her profession means she has to deal with lots of people. She made it clear from the beginning that she would support me always and unconditionally, but she had no desire to tread the political boards.

Of course, after the election nothing in her life was the same as before. Suddenly you discover you're the mayor's wife. You get invitations to all imaginable events. As the wife of the mayor of Reykjavík, one is a kind of First Lady of the nation. Ultimately, in Iceland there's only one city that's worthy of the name—and, consequently, only one mayor. (In this respect, Lady Gaga wasn't all that wrong when she appointed me to the post of "Mayor of Iceland.")

The activity of the mayor of Reykjavík is so extensive and so varied that it automatically seeps into one's private life. Every day runs on a fixed schedule, which is more or less drawn up by others. Moreover, anything and everything can happen in this job, and at any time the daily planning can go pear-shaped. Not to mention the work-related chronic stress. Also, I travel a lot, and my wife always has to be ready for my appointments getting in the way of her plans too. Being married to the mayor is a sort of part-time job in itself (voluntary and unpaid, of course).

My wife can manage, with only two days' notice, to rustle up a feast for three hundred people and turn it into an unforgettable experience for all concerned. In contrast, I can't even manage to organize a single day. I come up with an idea, forget what I'd planned the very next moment, and suddenly find myself doing something quite different. I head out of the house with my swimming bag because I have an appointment with someone in the hot tub, and as soon as I'm in the car, it seems to me the ideal time to do the shopping for dinner. And because I'm in the city anyway, I'll quickly pop the car over to the car wash. Leaving the shopping in the trunk.

In many ways, I'm just a normal man with normal strengths and weaknesses. Every now and then I'm also a genius. And at the same time I'm mentally retarded. I always find it difficult to adapt to new circumstances, which—given my spontaneous inspirations and my crackpot ideas—is of course not like me at all. So I'm basically just a walking contradiction with a strong tendency to chaos, and only Jóga knows how to introduce a little order into this chaos.

As a matter of principle, I never make any major decisions without talking with my wife about the potential impact on our family life. Outwardly I may often come across as hasty and inconsiderate, but in private I'm the exact opposite—extremely conscientious and circumspect. So it's often happened over time that my wife has played a more active part in my work than we had originally planned. She is my court of arbitration and also my closest collaborator. She also has some knowledge of the "internal" workings of the party.

My children didn't pay any attention to my election as mayor. On my youngest son, however, it had a direct impact. He was born in 2005, and as it happened he was just starting school as the Best Party was implementing its educational reforms. After the management of his former kindergarten attacked me sharply in an open letter, I decided to send the boy to a school that lay outside my jurisdiction. Even apart from that, he needed some time before he could make out what my new profession involved. At first he seemed to think of me as a kind of emperor who could do anything and everything he felt like doing, but eventually he realized that his father was just an ordinary man in an unusual job.

I was also surprised to see how many family members and distant relatives suddenly appeared out of the woodwork and asked me to do them some favor.

Every possible uncle, sister-in-law, and cousin suddenly wanted me to help them out with some trivial problem. And of course, my political decisions can have a concrete impact on people in my immediate sphere. Like when close relatives lose their jobs, or the jobs of friends and family members are rationalized into non-existence. Some of them are still pissed off at me.

I remember, for example, the extremely awkward situation that came about when we wanted to give a helping hand to the aforementioned ailing energy group Orkuveita Reykjavíkur. This bailout unfortunately entailed restructuring—i.e., layoffs. One of the victims was the father of Heiða, our party chairman. His entire department was closed down. Of course, Heiða had not planned to throw her own father out of work as a result of her party activities, but this kind of thing, unfortunately, can't always be prevented.

INTERVIEW WITH JÓHANNA (JÓGA) JÓHANNSDÓTTIR

Let's begin at the beginning. What are your recollections of the origins of the Best Party and Jón's campaign?

Jón making videos that were on YouTube in late 2009—"Simply the Best," seeming all full of himself—and then writing little articles and poking, poking. That was the start.

When did you realize that what he was doing was becoming more than just poking fun?

I thought it was a genius idea, especially when Jón thought of making a party out of it—a political party. I was the first member, the first member of his political party. And from then on, it was fun.

Jón has said that the Best Party didn't just happen overnight, but was "a product of many ideas—like ideas having sex and multiplying." From this the Best Party was born. I notice that it is viewed with

a certain mystery and respect; it was this phenom-enon, and you don't question it too much.

It was magical. And then to pick people, courageous people, artists, who were willing to work and be part of it and also . . . to tease. Because the situation was so serious in Iceland and none of us wanted more of the typical politicians that "know it all." So to push that to the limit—that's what we were after. But we didn't even know how to apply, how to start a political party. We didn't have any idea.

So, how does one start a political party?

You have to get people signing petitions for you, and you need a certain amount of signatures, and then you have to go to the City Hall and put down all that you have. Jón and Heiða did that, and from there on we were legal to do the campaign.

If the party was the product, the child, of all these ideas coming together, were you then the midwife and the mother alike?

Yeah, experienced mother and, yes, midwife—that's a good word for it. To give protection to the ideas and stop it when it was going too far and it wouldn't be healthy for the "child." Help bring it into the world.

Jón has said, "People don't realize it but the Best Party—a lot of it has to do with Jóga." Can you talk about what he meant—about the various roles you played and continue to play behind the scenes?

Some of it was just talking to the partners of people involved in the campaign. At first, some of them were like, "Forget it, no, my husband isn't going to go with that party." And I encouraged people to go for it.

How did you do that?

Because I believed it was necessary, it was needed, and it was an art piece, and it would be worth it. And I thought maybe at some point all the other politicians, they would wake up. That was my vision, from seeing in the middle—I thought they would say, "Okay, you're right, let's be human." Jón was doing such a great mirror image—holding up a mirror—to show them, to wake them up, to get them to be humble, and to be willing to take it on to another level. I was not thinking that Jón would end up as mayor and the whole party would end up there, but instead that they could wake them up—by art. By this art piece.

It does seem like it was art, like Dada art.

That's what it was. It was punk.

Which is part of who you are, too, right? Punk is part of your own history.

Yeah, and the punks are in their fifties now, and of course that age should take over. Why should they all be sixty and seventy and eighty years old? We all have responsibility to go into office, to serve—our generation.

Were there instances where you knew you needed certain kinds of expertise—say, an attorney, and you had to be like a casting director who had to find that person?

At one point, for instance, we needed someone who knew something about law. I knew one lawyer from twenty-five years back who also is a saxophone player and a real, genuine, living human being, but still a lawyer whom I trusted—and I made the call.

Was it difficult to persuade him?

He showed up one hour later. He just came and met us, and from there on he was on board.

As Jón's wife, you were very close to everything that was happening in the campaign, you were right in the middle of it day and night, but you also seem to have this ability to step back and see the big picture.

How did that ability help guide Jón and other members of the party in decision-making?

With me, I recognize geniuses, and I recognize genius ideas. It hits me. Jón is a genius. Then, all of these genius ideas he is getting, and all these other people also, so maybe that's why I'm like a good casting director—I can see them, I can pick them out. They are geniuses but with good hearts, and they're brave, and—this is key—they have what it takes to be on the frontline. They're singers, they're in a band, they know how to be onstage, which helps a lot.

But that's not my thing. I always love to help people go further, for their own mission. To see what suits them, what helps them to grow, and what's the next step to go a little bit out of their comfortable zone. I encourage them—"Go, go, go, go, go, go out of your comfort zone." In so many ways, it also has to do with the city, with the country, with Iceland. I want us all to go further. But it suits me to be in the background and supporting them. I love it when there are artists that can wake the mass up—the mass of people. I need to be somewhere supporting the people that can wake the mass up. Then I'm happy.

Another role you played was what I would call "energy conductor," helping to monitor the energy during the campaign—when to go full force, when to pull back, when to rest.

I'm like the bird. I have the view. Maybe it's needed when people are in a new situation, as all of them were at the time. Each and every one had their role. But it's difficult to have the view at the same time. So I was the one with the view.

Did you find yourself more having to tell them to pull back or to charge forward?

Go. More "go, go, go, go." Just a few times, I had to say to pull back and rest and not go into the dirty wrestling of politics. Get ready for when our opening was there to squeeze in—to walk in, not squeeze even—an opening of energy to go, go, go.

Someone who knows you very well said, "People instantly trust Jóga. They would jump off cliffs for her." But if this were so, I think you would jump first.

People trust me. I don't have a bad direction for people. I have a good heart.

If people are jumping off cliffs for you, then I would think they are jumping into a sea of love.

Well, they're jumping into something very interesting at least.

It might be a little choppy at times—

And fun, it's got to be fun. And something they probably thought they needed to do for a long time. I'm not pushing people. I'm more following and supporting the directions they want to go.

And that's certainly true of Jón and the campaign. You knew better probably than him that he needed to do this, that people needed for him to do this. I think one reason people may trust you so much is that you have this very powerful trust in instinct. You put it beautifully when you called it "loyalty to the force."

Yes, that's how I feel. You must have "loyalty to the force," the energy.

I was interested to know that your father was a sailor, and you traveled with him a lot.

He was on container ships, sailing from Iceland through all Europe. I went with him on many, many trips, from the time I was about six years old. This had a lot to do with shaping who I am, learning probably more than I know from all of these sailors, and being sometimes the only girl on board—seven years old, eight years old—and being allowed to work with my dad for two weeks. I was always doing something—helping the guys out painting, or helping the cook, or doing dishes. To be part of the crew. I was very young, but I was part of the crew.

**And here, years later, you were part of the crew
with the Best Party, but maybe your role was also
serving as the compass—making sure that it was
headed the right way.**

Yes, helping to direct the ship. Plus you learn from
sailing that sometimes there are forces out of your
control, like the weather, things that you can't control.

**Were there moments during the campaign when
you felt forces out of your control, and you just had
to ride with it?**

At one point, yes, when it was out of our hands, it was
the brutality of politics. I think only once I said, "Now
we have to stop, we are not going to go into the mud."
Brutal mud-slinging: Jón was "the Clown," and didn't
deserve to be there, and so on. I didn't want hurt for
my people. So I said we had to stop, to pull back.

**Why do you think people responded so positively
to Jón?**

Jón is simply a good man. What makes a good man
is good intentions for all, and that he has always had.
Also, he had been on the radio for many years, he
was known. People see when there is a great stand-
up comedian and recognize the intellect; it's the very

intellectual people who can make fun and look deep, deep, deep. Also, Jón wrote articles in the paper about life and various topics, these were collected in a book, and he gave lectures. One thing he would say, which was great, was, "Service is the highest love." So people got to know him. And none of the politicians were really aware of how well known he was, other than being a clown. They saw the clown as a silly person, not an intellectual.

So people recognized that Jón had that sincere side to him.

Iceland is so small, so even if you were not at the lecture or didn't know him, then perhaps the third person from you had been and would tell you how sincere he was.

While the name of the party, the Best Party, was in fun, there was also truth to it, and a real desire to make things the best they could be.

Still we use the word every day: "This is bad, but that is best." It's just simple. If we have to make a decision— should we go for the bad, or should we go for the best? There's your answer.

He has said that the campaign was about politics, but that being mayor is about common sense.

Common sense, communication, wanting the best. No one has left the Best Party—we're all still part of it. Like in a good band, we're used to everyone having a say, to ping-pong an idea between the drummer, for instance, and the other band members, anyone having something to say about the song. Everyone has a voice.

So, being in City Hall is almost like being in a band.

Yes, to get the best idea out of it. In the end, where does it come from? You can't really tell—it comes from the band as a whole.

It seems that this sense of play is an important part of the campaign, and an important part of you. I especially notice how often you use the word "giggle"—

It's so needed. Life is too serious. And for me, it's light—when there's a giggle, or compassion, tears, there is light. And that's what I count on. There were so many giggles during the campaign, it was constant giggling bursting out again and again and again.

That must have been infectious—were people throughout Reykjavík enjoying the giggle too?

Yes, they giggled with us, and they were willing at least to have a giggle for the next four years. Just at least have a giggle. We don't have money. Everything had been boring. People love to giggle. I mean, what is better than having a good laugh? A spontaneous laugh. Nothing feels better—when you laugh so hard that you're crying. Then you're on top—the light is shining. And I have a theory also about the light and the dark. The dark, for me, is confusion; darkness is confusion. So when there's laughter and moving forward, little steps, running—at least you're going forward. You're in light. That's what everybody deserves.

I imagine you have learned many unexpected things over the past three years.

It has been a university for me. It has been great, and difficult at times. It will leave us worn out, that's for sure, but it has given more—given to all of us. It will leave us with a free education, a surprise education—on human behavior, on how cities run. For example, when it's snowing we start thinking about money. The snowflake was always beautiful for me. I have always loved the snow. But now, when it's snowing, I'm thinking, "It's going to cost so much to clear the streets." So we have a different view, which is healthy and so much fun. No matter where we are in our lives, whatever city we're in, from now on we will always have this view from City Hall.

Interview by Bill Hayes

FACEBOOK AND CO.

Ever since I discovered it for myself, the Internet has fascinated me. It is, in my view, the most decisive invention in human history since the discovery of fire. I'm actually always on the Net, always surfing, from here to there and back again. I was one of the first IRC users in Iceland. And I love Facebook. It's just such fun to share stuff on Facebook with people, or follow their activities. I've also used Facebook to spread my views.

But since I've been mayor, Facebook has lost its entertainment value for me. My contacts with my Facebook friends are not the same as before, though I can't say exactly why that is so. Maybe the others have suddenly gotten self-conscious. In any case, this break can't be denied, and I think that's a crying shame. It's as if an invisible wall has slid between me and other people. Only now and then do I get a private message, sometimes even from old friends—who were probably sitting slumped in front of their computer with a bottle of red wine and suddenly felt the need to tell me something.

My real Facebook profile runs under a pseudonym and is accessible to only my very best friends. In addition, I have five fictitious identities. For example,

I'm an older woman who comes off as pretty open-minded and positive. Then I'm an Icelandic captain who works for the North Korean airline Air Koryo, a British guy living alone in Kingston-upon-Hull, and a dim, untalented but avid hobby photographer. And finally, I'm a bitter gay man who has retired from society and bunkered down in a summer house somewhere in the country where he wants to live in harmony with nature; he hangs around all day on news portals and dating forums. All of these people also have masses of Facebook friends, who of course also do not exist. Only a few know who is behind all the imaginary figures.

It's still a lot of fun to have my say through these people. For example, if someone sends me a link to some caustic comment about me, then the lively, open-minded lady immediately arrives on the scene and defends me and my position.

Apart from these fake identities I run two regular Facebook pages: The one, called "Diary of a Mayor," is mostly about the City of Reykjavík and urban issues. And then there is the homepage of the public person Jón Gnarr. This site is entirely in English and serves to spread my thoughts and views beyond the borders of Iceland.

STRESS

Soon after I took office, the dark forces of the Icelandic political scene began to sharpen their claws. Much of what I've done in office has been the focus of criticism; my person and every word that came out of my mouth was derided and mocked. When I refused to receive the officers of a German warship, this was interpreted not as the statement of a committed pacifist, but as an insult to a friendly nation.

I have fought all my life to be allowed to change my name. There are various personal reasons for this. I was born Jón Gunnar Kristinsson, but not since my childhood have I actually been called by that name. My early years are associated with painful memories. Since I was fourteen I've called myself Jón Gnarr. Jón Gunnar Kristinsson was a neglected little boy who was thought to be backward. Jón Gnarr, on the other hand, is an optimistic, creative, sincere, and courageous adult. Due to the rigid Icelandic laws on individuals' names, I could never succeed in getting my name officially changed. This too has been exploited by my political adversaries, who, as a matter of principle, call me Jón Gunnar Kristinsson or Jón G. Kristinsson.

At first I was afraid that this group would pounce on my family and take apart my private life—an extremely disturbing idea. But strangely enough, that never happened. At most indirectly. Of course, it still hurts my family when nasty stories are spread about me.

An example: In the third year of my term in office, I spent my summer holidays in Norway. I was there for two weeks visiting my sister who lives with her husband and children there. I get to see her all too seldom. Meanwhile, back home in Iceland, the SUS, the youth organization of the Independents, had started a manhunt for me, and the Conservative mouthpiece *Morgunblaðið* printed the same message on its front page, declared that I was missing, and also started searching for me. It was all pure harassment, of course. They knew very well that I was just on holiday. I didn't think I owed anyone an explanation.

My job keeps me on the go right round the clock, such that I can hardly find the time to see my own children and close relatives. I'm already out of the house when my youngest gets up and starts getting ready for school, and when I come home in the evening he's already getting ready for bed.

When my father died, my mother moved into a nursing home. Shortly before Christmas 2010, when I'd been in office for just seven months, she got pneumonia, and then went downhill fast. She died on the first day of the Christmas holiday. At this moment my whole life imploded. I was chronically exhausted, worn out and worn down by the constant hostility. I felt as if I was falling to pieces inside. I would like to have simply vamoosed, crawled into some hole, pulled the earth over me, and disappeared.

What came next was sadness, pain, and depression. Nevertheless, I somehow managed not to show it outwardly. In reality, I was constantly on the verge of collapse, but this was one favor I didn't want to do for my enemies, and that idea kept me afloat. I threw myself into my work with zeal, and took each day as it came. When I was overcome with longing for my mother, I took her make-up things out, put on her lipstick, and painted my fingernails with her nail polish.

It was clear from the beginning that this job would in the long run ruin my health. Constant strain, stress, and lack of sleep can all permanently weaken the immune system. I've ended up in the hospital twice, and my migraines aren't getting any better. For social contacts outside of work, in any case, I have little time and energy, and the few hours' free time that remain mine, I spend with my family. Still, so far I've never been unhappy, just tired. Boundlessly tired, not to say pretty much at the end of my tether.

The world of television fascinated me from an early age. Even as a child I was completely familiar with it and have always raved about certain movies and series. But since I've been mayor, this has completely vanished from my life. Since then, TV has been more or less a no-no, as I simply lack the time to watch it.

Also, I sometimes begin to wonder whether, after all these complex tasks and responsible decisions, after all the deaths in the family, the smear campaigns and permanent hostility, I'll ever be able to do comedy again.

I'm often asked where and how I actually chill out, how I recharge my batteries. The answer: I spend an hour every day just by myself. This time is sacred to me. Then I take the dog for a walk and listen to something relaxing.

I've gotten involved in a complicated project and I'm still in the thick of it. At the moment I can't look back and assess the overall picture, the scope of the whole. But I'm working on it day by day, and if I'm honest, I know I've been counting the days right from the start.

I'm often asked if being mayor has changed me in any way. Whether this position has made me a different person. The answer is a plain and simple no. It's really not changed me at all. Of course, I've become more mature, have learned on the job, and understand a few things better than before. But as far as my character goes, that's not changed in the slightest. I'm neither frustrated nor offended nor bitter, and don't bear anyone any grudges. Not even those who have made my life difficult.

What most distinguishes the office of mayor, more than anything else, is fatigue. I've never been so tired in my life. And I already got tired quite frequently. My youngest son was very ill in his early years, and during that time I was in a state of constant worry and never got much sleep. But never before have I experienced such abysmal, leaden fatigue as in this job. A weariness that pervades the whole body. That spreads everywhere, in the toes, in the heart and brain, in the arms, in the dick. Fatigue in the ears, in the eyes. In the skin.

After a few months in office, I had the spontaneous idea of having the coat of arms of the city of Reykjavík tattooed on my underarm—as visible proof that I took my job seriously and identified completely with my city. But apparently I had been a little remiss in terms of hygiene, with the result that the tattoo promptly got infected. For a while I gritted my teeth, pretended there was nothing wrong, and hoped it would heal up by itself. But then, at a conference in Sweden, I collapsed with severe pain and a high temperature and ended up in a Stockholm hospital with blood poisoning and a harsh infection. I flew home, where I was admitted to the state hospital and put on a drip, with antibiotics being fed directly into the vein. The doctor spoke of acute stress, and said something like that could easily cripple the entire immune system.

Of course, being mayor also has a very direct

impact on my private and family life. As these jobs always do. My working day usually lasts from eight to five, in the evening emails have to be answered, reports read, and the weekends are given up to receptions and various other commitments. Apparently, there are politicians who like to show up in public with their children. I myself try to limit this to an absolute minimum. I take my youngest son with me if it's something really fun and exciting, or if he asks specifically. But here in the city administration, for example, there's nothing of interest for him.

Sometimes I am overcome by boundless sadness and despair, and then, much to the displeasure of my staff, I give in to my unrestrained self-pity. My head feels like it's just about to burst, and I have the feeling I've gotten myself into something that I will never understand, not even partly. Then I long for my old life. It's far from easy to retain your optimism and sense of humor.

I've already set up all kinds of things in my life— I've invented, written, and concocted plays, skits, TV series, and books—but I think the Best Party is just about the most brilliant thing I've managed to do so far. I have shown courage, inventiveness, and creativity. Where this energy comes from, I don't exactly know. I'm always happy when my person or the city of Reykjavík get good press in foreign media, because then I feel that what I'm doing here has a deeper meaning. I do not believe in God or an afterlife. But I'm a damn tough representative of our species. If I were an animal I'd probably be a polar bear. Perhaps I am directly descended from the Neanderthals. Maybe I just have a Neanderthal gene that keeps me moving.

REYKJAVÍK—CITY OF PEACE

Iceland is a peaceful country. It has no army and no armed police. We have instead a centuries-old tradition of solving conflicts not with weapons, but with words. We have relied on it from day one—if only to survive on this island.

I wish you could simply extirpate violence and war from the world, abolish all the armed forces, and destroy all the bombs. But this is probably not very realistic. Ultimately, everyone has to start with themselves. Many want to be active somewhere else, at best in a country where they don't currently live. But what's the point, if there is no peace in your own life? So be at peace with yourself. And how? Through peaceful dealings with others. Start by ensuring peace at home before you go out into the world. Or work for peace in both spheres. You can't be working for a peace camp in the Middle East during the day and then in the evening have a quarrel with your family over the phone.

Of course we must start somewhere, geographically, if we wish to commit ourselves to peace. In my view, Reykjavík is ideally suited as a starting point for this work. When Reagan and Gorbachev shook hands here in 1986, thus sealing the end of the Cold War and the grotesque arms race between the superpowers, Reykjavík was catapulted into the focus of world attention. Every year, thousands of tourists dedicated to peace come here as pilgrims to visit the site of that historic handshake, the venerable urban reception villa of Höfði.

I have set myself the goal of supporting the culture of peace in Reykjavík and advancing its development as the "City of Peace." I dream that the name Reykjavík will one day be associated with peace throughout the world, that our city will, in peace building and human rights, eventually lead the world and serve as a model for other cities. A few foundations have already been laid.

Even now, the city of Reykjavík is associated with various peace and human rights projects—for example "Mayors for Peace," a global network that was founded in 1982 on the initiative of the mayors of Hiroshima and Nagasaki, and with the support of the United Nations. The member cities are committed to humanitarian tasks such as refugee protection and the fight against hunger and poverty in the world, but first and foremost they pursue the abolition of all nuclear weapons by the year 2020. This may be considered naive, but in my opinion such a goal is worth every attempt.

In addition, Reykjavík has for some years been a member of ICORN, the International Cities of Refuge Network, which offers politically persecuted writers and poets asylum, shelter, and a protected space for writing. In this framework, in autumn 2011 we were able to welcome our first guest, the Palestinian poet Mazen Maarouf. In summer 2012, Reykjavík was the venue for an extraordinary conference that, under the title "The Spirit of Humanity Forum," drew people from all over the world to Iceland to exchange their ideas for a better and more peaceful future. We as planners and initiators would like to continue to grow this annual forum and hope that the event—like the World Economic Forum in Davos—will gradually become a become an established event.

On the island of Viðey in the bay of Reykjavík stands the Imagine Peace Tower, Yoko Ono's "peace column." This impressive light installation is lit up annually on October 9, the birthday of John Lennon. It emits its gigantic beam of light into the sky until December 8, the day of his assassination. Yoko Ono usually travels to this event in person. The pillar of light has now become an integral part of cultural life in Reykjavík. Every other year, within the same framework, the international peace prize known as the Lennon/Ono Grant for Peace is awarded—a ceremony that I have already been able to attend twice. Give Peace a Chance.

The residents of Reykjavík are very well aware of the special position of our city in an international context. But the image of the picturesque colorful toy town is no longer enough. Now it's time to get down to business. We should start by marketing Reykjavík as a city of peace, as an international center for conferences, forums, and everything else that has to do with peace and human rights work.

Those who want peace must open their mouths wider than others. Peace is a basic human right, and as long as wars are still being waged around the world, we cannot in good conscience count ourselves to be worthy members of the highly civilized species Homo sapiens. We should set ourselves the goal of establishing specific peace zones, and expanding and extending them over the whole world. Peace must not just be the privilege of a few nations: it is the right of every individual. And if we want to enforce this right, it depends on every individual. On all of us. Silence is not enough. What matters now is that all sorts of people—those in public life, celebrities, people in leadership positions, mayors, presidents, politicians, and everyone else— take the initiative.

I have been an active member of Amnesty International for many years. When I became mayor, it would have been the obvious decision to take a break from this commitment while in office. Everyone would have understood that. But instead, I decided to commit myself even more and use my position in a very specific way. I am always happy to make the fact known in public, to take part in petitions and rallies, and I'm always there when Amnesty organizes any protests. In talks with foreign guests, I speak out clearly against human rights violations in their respective countries, especially when it comes to capital punishment or nuclear proliferation—of course, I always make my points in a polite manner. Most people lend a surprisingly sympathetic ear.

Recently, the City Council of Moscow passed a law making Gay Pride parades in public a punishable offense. Thereupon, I addressed a letter to the mayor of Moscow—which was, after all, one of our partner cities!—protesting against this decision. I asked him to lift this unjust and completely absurd ban and instead use the influence of his position to support lesbians and gays in their struggle for a decent life.

In terms of homosexual equality, Iceland is probably a world leader. The citizens of Reykjavík are immensely proud of Reykjavík Pride, the Hinsegin dagar, now the largest city and street party of the year. I myself have been actively involved in it almost every year, and since I've been mayor (and I am particularly proud of this) I have even made it my trademark to wave down to the crowd from garishly decorated floats, dressed in changing drag costumes.

The year before last I had planned to get dolled up as Princess Leia. Everything was ready: costume, wig, and props. But less than two hours before the start of the parade, I had the spontaneous idea instead of pulling on a Pussy Riot mask to express my solidarity with the Russian punk rock band.

INTERNATIONAL POLITICS

As mayor, I'd like to remain true to myself. I'm trying to do my job as well as my conscience will allow. I take the trouble to go into the nitty-gritty of complicated situations, even if I find them basically dead boring. At all costs, I want to avoid inflicting any damage on our city through negligence, thoughtlessness, or sloth. On the other hand, it's vital for me to have fun, and if I think of something hysterically funny, then I try to implement it. For example, appearing at official occasions in weird clothing or posting oblique comments on Facebook.

Politicians abroad are not generally aware of me. I know, for example, that Obama has been informed about the Best Party, but obviously this news has not made him fall off his chair. Certainly, Iceland is a small country, sparsely populated and far away, which is probably why foreign politicians tend to overlook or dismiss me as a naive buffoon.

My protest letter to the Mayor of Moscow, in which I criticized the ban on Gay Pride parades, was formulated with exquisite politeness. I have yet to receive an answer. I've also written to Obama, describing my ideas about Reykjavík as the "City of Peace" and asking him to keep us in mind as a locale for international peace gatherings. This letter I wrote to him as the most powerful man in the world, but also as a winner of the Nobel Peace Prize. I got no reaction from the White House either.

In my role as Mayor of Reykjavík, I regularly deal with Scandinavian politicians. These contacts are always nice and friendly, without them showing me or the Best Party any appreciable interest or seeking to have any personal conversation with me. The only political groups who wanted to know more about me were the Greens in Austria and the German Pirate Party. Maybe I spook foreign politicians a bit. They can't anticipate what new crazy idea I'm going to come up with next and are scared that my antics might encourage people in their own countries to mimic me.

The only prominent intellectual who seems to have a genuine interest in me is the linguist and political maven Noam Chomsky. Chomsky makes no secret of the fact that he thinks I'm the best mayor ever—which of course is a great honor to me. When he was in Reykjavík as a guest, we met here at City Hall for a fruitful exchange of ideas, and since then we've stayed in touch.

At international conferences people generally place me with the Left, more or less. That said, I'm not inevitably invited to the compulsory dinner receptions, and when I am, it's mainly thanks to representatives of grassroots movements who want to meet me. This has often led, both in Europe and in the States, to thrilling encounters, such as with people from the inner circles of the Occupy Wall Street movement. These contacts were, for whatever reason, never permanent, but I am neither bitter nor eaten up with resentment.

My contacts with representatives of other countries such as China, Russia, and the United States were always pleasant and uncomplicated. All of these ambassadors and consuls general have shown me respect and friendship. I had a particularly good rapport with the U.S. Ambassador, Mr. Luis Arreaga, who took up his post here at about the same time I took office—a really nice guy.

After the parliamentary elections in Italy in 2013, when the party of Beppe Grillo was able to win its legendary success, a few Italian politicians got in touch with me. Beppe Grillo himself and, not least, the people in his immediate circle had announced that I'd always been a driving force and a kind of role model for them and their party.

But of course I'm not a politician. I just got involved in politics. Now you might well say that as soon as you stand in a democratic election and get elected you're a politician. I don't know if I would agree with that. All in all, I'm probably something a bit like the Mars rover *Curiosity*. A reconnaissance vehicle on a distant planet. Is *Curiosity* a Martian? Did he become a Martian when he landed on Mars? How long do you have to spend on Mars before you can count as a Martian? These are good questions.

A LETTER TO BARACK OBAMA

Jón Gnarr's letter to President Obama, dated November 19, 2012.

Dear Mr. President,

I sincerely congratulate you and your family on your victory in the U.S. presidential election. The people of Reykjavík followed the elections with great interest and the majority of Icelanders were on your side.

Everything is going pretty well here in the City of Reykjavík after a few difficult years. The city is full of life and the atmosphere is positive. Recently, Reykjavík was designated as a UNESCO City of Literature, the fifth city in the world, and the first non-native-English-speaking city to receive this title. This was a great honor for our city because Icelanders see themselves as a nation of literature.

Iceland is also a peaceful nation, without an army, and I am eager to make Reykjavík a completely military free zone. I have a dream that Reykjavík could, in the future, become a center for peace and human rights in the world. As you know, Ronald Reagan and Mikhail Gorbachev held a remarkable meeting here in the Höfði House in the year 1986, which defined the end of the Cold War.

The unique art installation by the Japanese artist Yoko Ono, the Imagine Peace Tower, is located on Videy Island in Reykjavík. Every year, from the 9th of October until the 8th of December, it shines in the sky with the Aurora Borealis, reminding us of Yoko and John's hope for world peace.

I believe it is important for our city to recognize our obligation and contribute to promoting peace. Reykjavík is in a unique position to be a city of peace, and I'd like to suggest that you have our city in mind if you need a place for a meeting, peace negotiation, conference for peace, etc.

In the year 1972, Bobby Fischer and Boris Spassky met in Reykjavík to play chess. The match attracted more worldwide interest than any other chess match before or since. Bobby Fischer moved to Iceland in 2005 and he lived here until his death in 2008. He suffered from personal difficulties during the last few years of his life and is buried at Laugardælakirkjugarður in Iceland.

Reykjavík and the United States have a good relationship. The U.S. Embassy in Reykjavík has truly achieved success in its work. The ambassador, the honorable Luis E. Arreaga, is an active participant in the cultural life of our city and is a very admirable representative of the USA. Seattle and Reykjavík are sister cities, and Seattle was a special guest of honor at our last Culture Night, which is one of our city's main events. We also received a visit from the city council of Denver last summer, when Icelandair launched direct flights between our cities.

If I can assist you or your great country in any way, do not hesitate to contact me; send me an e-mail or call, and I will be at your service.

I know that you are a very busy man, but if you are ever on the move it would be a pleasure and an honor to have the opportunity to meet with you and tell you about my ideas regarding our special city, Reykjavík. Please feel free to drop by for a cup of coffee, we have an airport in the middle of the city. Last year, your grandmother, Sarah, came to Iceland. Unfortunately, I didn't have the opportunity to meet her at that time, but she is doing a very good job indeed.

I hope you are in good health and I wish you every success in the future.

Regards,
Jón Gnarr,
The Mayor of Reykjavík

P.S. I know you're a big fan of *The Wire*, and so am I. I had the honor to meet Clarke Peters (Lester Freamon) when he was in Iceland this summer to participate in the Spirit of Humanity Forum peace conference.

NATO

On March 30, 1949, the Icelandic Althingi, despite strong protests from the population, signed Iceland's accession to NATO. I never understood what Iceland had to do with NATO. For decades, the U.S. Army had its military base in Keflavík—until they realized in 2006 that there was actually nothing for them to do here, whereupon they packed their bags and left. As it stands, our NATO membership means that if we are attacked, someone will defend us. But who's going to attack us? And what for? Suppose North Korea invaded Iceland. Would our friends in the States and Europe leave us in the lurch just because we haven't paid our annual membership fee?

I am unconditionally for Iceland's withdrawal from NATO. Sure, NATO is a necessary organization in many ways, and I can understand why the Americans, French, Germans, and other military nations want to belong. But what has Iceland got to do with this club? Therefore, I am of the opinion that we should find a way to tactfully and discreetly leave this organization.

As we are currently in NATO, military aircraft and warships are regularly stationed here, either to refuel or simply to pay us an internal NATO courtesy visit.

Shortly after I took office, I learned that it is tradition-ally expected of the mayor that he invite the officers of foreign warships to a ceremonial reception at the Town Hall. I then explained that there would not be any such receptions under me, and that I had no inten-tion of taking up any reciprocal invitations. On the other hand, I very frequently visit warships that are used as training ships or coastal rescue craft. As far as I know, the people in charge of these ships fully un-derstand my position. Now I am looking for a way of keeping the rest of the navies away from Iceland and letting them maneuver to other ports.

Furthermore, the domestic airport in Reykjavík is widely used for military purposes, as a staging post for military aircraft, and by the American secret service, for example, which uses this airport for prisoner trans-ports. I have put in a formal request to our government to stop any type of military use of the airport, and the agreement banning it has already been signed. But strangely enough, it seems to have had no effect so far.

Nature, culture, peace, and humanity, these are the fixed points in my life—as mayor, but also and above all as a human being. I dream of being able to declare one day that Reykjavík is a 100 percent military-free zone. Attentiveness and respect for others, for family, friends, and all the people around us, are the basis of any society. A sense of humanity is also high on the list, because without humanity everything else is futile: religions, political movements, or anything else at all.

THE WORLD IS GETTING BETTER AND BETTER

Contrary to what many believe, I think the world is getting better. There are fewer wars, and humankind is developing increasingly effective, sophisticated methods to create and secure peace. The future belongs to democracy, but how well this democracy functions depends on how many of us actively participate in it. If there are too few, democracy is flat and banal. If a mass movement springs into being, this in turn runs the risk of being cumbersome and costly.

Of course democracy can also be as boring as hell. We all know what they're like, those meetings that always seem to take place after work or on weekends and are known havens for oddballs of every kind whose main priority is basking in the glory of their own words, rather than contributing anything to the discussion.

Ever since I've been in office, I've organized numerous public meetings and information evenings that were meant to give people some definite ideas, plans, or concepts, and then answer any questions they might have about the relevant project. You can bet your bottom dollar that sooner or later, some old fraud will turn up who monopolizes the proceedings and, instead of asking a simple question, bores everyone present to tears with a long-winded review of his life. Eventually the chair will interrupt and ask if he wants to ask a specific question, so the guy says yes, babbles on and, after ten or fifteen minutes, gradually comes to a conclusion that does not, however, produce any question, but loses itself in general, circuitous considerations about God and the world.

The biggest snag with democracy is that stupid people have as much right as intelligent people to express an opinion and that, of course, you have to treat the yokels respectfully. By "yokels" I don't necessarily mean people who are a bit simple-minded or mentally handicapped. I'm talking about those who are ill-prepared and are much more interested in showing themselves off than in making a decent contribution to the public good or finding the solution to a problem.

Is it any wonder that the younger generation is usually conspicuous in its absence from such meetings? Why would you discuss something that you think is relevant in a closed group of fifty to one hundred people when you could spread the exact same thing on Facebook or Twitter and thus reach thousands? Plus block undesirable blabbermouths with one click.

The politics of the future is local politics—urban and district affairs. This does not mean that public, democratic meetings are a thing of the past—but they have to be set up differently. The citizens' meeting of today is a targeted, professionally well-founded exchange of thoroughly prepared participants who consequently achieve the desired goals. Citizens' democracy is still just as important as direct democracy: we need both, because both are essential to life.

In ancient Athens, for instance, direct democracy worked outstandingly well—every single citizen was allowed to comment on each question and cast his vote. Apart from the fact, of course, that women and slaves were left out of it, the ancient Greeks had one of the most advanced forms of democracy. Although only about five thousand of the approximately forty thousand inhabitants of Athens were actively involved, this example shows that direct democracy can work if a certain percentage of citizens is ready to invest their time and energy. And people must also recognize the value of this personal involvement. It is also interesting that comedians played a major role in Attic democracy and decisively influenced the formation of opinion among the people.

If we want to reform our democracy today and improve it overall, we are dependent on the Internet. Only by digital means can we sustainably make any difference on this point—while limiting cost and time to a minimum.

In this sense, the online platform Betri Reykjavík,

which we presented to the public in October 2011 in Reykjavík city center, is a small revolution. It comes from the think tank of Gunnar Grimsson and Róbert Bjarnason, two talented computer nerds, and links an information pool containing material on the different city districts with a thematically organized idea exchange in which each and every person can participate. Since its activation, the website has received numerous awards at home and abroad, including the "Icelandic Internet Prize" for the most original and interesting website, and also—as the first Icelandic participant— the international "World eDemocracy Award" for 2011. Meanwhile, the portal has been online for a good two years and is enjoying ever-increasing popularity and participation.

As is well known, consideration of plans and projects in your own district can cause tempers to flare. On Betri Reykjavík you can find all the important information on such issues at a glance. You can read the ideas, opinions, and suggestions of others, discuss the proposed concept, present your own ideas, and then vote for or against. Instead of spending two hours in some stuffy office down in the city, drinking vending-machine coffee and listening to vacuous anecdotes about some employee's private life, you can sit comfortably at home, in peace and quiet, at your computer, in your underwear if you feel like it, and within ten minutes you'll get feedback to your questions. The possibilities opened up by such a portal are almost inexhaustible, and accordingly the success of Betri Reykjavík has been making waves even in Parliament.

In addition, we have introduced direct elections for construction projects and renovation work in the various parts of the city—the first digitally conducted citizens' elections in Iceland. Voters sign in with their personal data, log into their account, and cast their vote. This election process, in a sense a first step towards "participatory budgeting," opens up entirely new paths and perspectives.

Unfortunately, however, not even direct digital democracy is a guarantee against lobbying and corruption. Large stakeholders and organizations can still feather their own nests with impunity—except that this now happens on the open stage rather than in secret wheeling and dealing behind the closed doors of some back room. Transparent corruption, so to speak. If the suspicion should arise that something isn't quite right, it is of course up to each individual to dig deeper and take the persons concerned to task. To get people to assume responsibility themselves in this simple way is basically no more complicated than encouraging them to sort out their garbage for recycling. They just have to understand the principle and recognize the benefit of their contribution. It is perfectly legitimate to apply a certain pressure and, for example, threaten to abolish this opportunity for participation if the turnout slips below a certain percentage.

These may be subtle points that only become real

when they are actually put into execution, but as a rule they work extremely well: Those who refuse to sort out their garbage, or are simply too lazy to do so, first receive a few friendly phone calls. And if that doesn't work, their trash cans are simply no longer emptied.

REPRESSION

For me, a person is first and foremost a person. Nationality, ethnic origin, gender, and sexual orientation are all one to me. People are people. Not that I'm saying that I'm completely free of prejudice. Prejudices are probably just as human as anything else. From the information it gets, a brain draws certain conclusions in order to protect its owner from threats. If this information is limited, the conclusions turn out to be pretty obvious.

In my life, I've already had to deal with the most varied sorts of people. With people of all nationalities, men and women, gays and lesbians, people with transgender identity. I would never even think of placing them within any rigid, judgmental categories. With the best will in the world, I can't discover anything in these people that would allow them to be divided up like that. Certainly not based on externals such as appearance, clothing style, political or religious beliefs, and the like.

On July 7, 2005, the date on which the bombings in the London Underground hit the news worldwide, I happened to be staying in London myself. For days and weeks afterwards, the city seemed paralyzed; the fear, insecurity, and mistrust were palpable. The perpetrators were young, radical Islamists, and there is one scene in particular that I'll never forget: I was sitting in the Underground, when suddenly a young man got in, apparently of Arabic origin, wearing a small backpack over his shoulder. My heart began to race. My first impulse was to get off at the next station and take another train, one without Arabs. But that would have been ridiculous, so I stayed where I was, a bundle of tension, mistrust, and fear. What if the guy had an explosive device in his backpack? I tried to push my way inconspicuously through the other passengers to increase the distance between him and me. If he suddenly started yelling "Allah Akhbar" through the train compartment, I'd simply throw myself to the floor between the rows of seats.

I must note that I wasn't the only passenger to react that way. The young Arab soon stood alone at the far end of the compartment with plenty of room around him, even though the Tube was jam packed. Everyone involuntarily kept their distance. And that is prejudice. The natural protective response of the brain to a presumed imminent danger. To my great relief, the backpack carrier didn't have a bomb. He got out at the same station as me and strolled quietly away.

Afterwards, I was a bit ashamed, but now I've come to terms with it and tell myself that it was a natural human reaction. People come in countless different types, and that's the fascinating thing about human culture and society.

But why do people use these superficial criteria to reprimand their fellow human beings? I assume that, here again, our innate, deep-rooted need for security lies behind it. In other words: in familiar surroundings we feel most at home, where everyone looks like us, acts like us, and thinks like us, where we always know more or less what to expect. In this way, prejudices are simply relics of our primitive nature, and thus completely normal.

This is where selfishness comes into play. When we smell a chance to exploit others for our own interests, we want to take this opportunity. I'm not at all trying to defend this—I try to resist such temptation as much as possible—but I can understand it very well. I understand which internal forces are at work. I understand why women are oppressed in some countries and are treated as second-class citizens, why they have no rights, and are patronized, pushed around, and forced to submit to rigid, arbitrary rules. I find all this fundamentally wrong and deeply despicable. But I can understand it. Men want to limit women's power as much as possible, out of pure selfishness of course, to exploit them more easily for their sexual interests. This works particularly well in the religious sphere.

There's just one thing that will probably always remain a mystery to me: homophobia, as it is called. In my eyes this is the greatest conceivable aberration. *Phobia* comes from the Greek and means "fear." Anyone who suffers from arachnophobia is afraid of spiders. Perfectly understandable. "Homophobia" on the other hand is an entirely different matter. This is not about people who once upon a time in their youth stumbled into a gay bar, got the fright of their lives, and have never managed to put the trauma behind them. The vast majority of those so-called homophobes are what are generally referred to as Philistines. Therefore, homophobia is not a phobia, but stupidity and intolerance. And most of all selfishness. These people have simply cobbled together an abstruse worldview, or some naive theory about life, God, the world, and all the rest of it.

What do I care if my neighbor is gay or not? Not a bean. Nor if he's into collecting dolls in traditional costume. In my view, a lesbian woman is just as normal as one who smokes a pipe. I just find it fascinating how different people are, and I cannot understand for the life of me what is supposed to be "unnatural," in other words "against the will of nature," about lesbians and gay men. Such a view is already complete garbage, as nature itself has no will, let alone any plans or intentions. But Mother Nature is open to the widest variety of characteristics, peculiarities, and different types, and what can't preserve itself is sorted out again by selection. As we know, homosexuality can be proven to have existed since earliest prehistory and is therefore a natural and integral part of evolutionary history. If it went against the laws of nature, then nature itself would long since have eradicated it, and it would be as extinct today as many other natural phenomena, from the dinosaurs to the Neanderthals.

To grant to same-sex couples fewer rights than those granted to every other couple is just about as absurd as banning a white man from living with a black woman. This was indeed once verboten, or at least frowned upon, in many parts of the world. The same evolution will happen with attitudes to homosexuality. When I see rallies at which people fight bitterly against the equality of gays and lesbians, I can't help thinking back to the unrest in the American South at the beginning of the last century, when backward hillbillies protested against the equality of blacks.

If you sit at home in your living room brooding about whether the guy next door is gay or the woman who lives on the floor below you is a pipe-smoker or your boss collects dolls in traditional costume, then you should seek professional help.

The same is true for transgender people of every variation, cross-dressers, drag kings, and drag queens. This gender diversity, too, is completely natural, and is incredibly creative in the way it is lived. Since I've been aware, I've had a weakness for women's clothes—and for an actor and comedian, of course, this is a definite plus. Styling myself as a woman has quite a liberating impact on me.

Where this costume mania comes from, I can't exactly say. I grew up almost exclusively among women. My mother and her sisters were my main caregivers.

Dad was usually at work, and when he did come home, he usually went around in his uniform. Many people claim they can easily recognize the different types of women in my repertoire. My sister, for example, finds it tremendously hard to watch me in female roles on stage, because she thinks she's watching herself. I really just use their words and body language—these are already in my blood.

When my mother died, I went through a severe identity crisis. It was as if something essential, part of my inner being, had suddenly been cut out of my life. I not only lost contact with my "roots," but also with a part of myself that seemed to have died with her. Eventually, I realized that it was actually the other way around: a part of me did not die with her, but a part of her lived on in me.

When we started going through her belongings, I absolutely wanted to keep her makeup stuff. In the weeks after her death, I kept having the sudden need to put on her lipstick and use her nail polish. A few times, I even popped into a meeting or a City Hall debate with painted lips and painted nails. Many people recoiled at this or thought it was inappropriate, but for me it was a completely natural expression of how much I missed Mom.

This has absolutely nothing to do with my sexual identity. Wearing women's clothes has no sexual component for me. Of course, I fully understand people for whom this is the case, because they've been born in the wrong body; women who feel imprisoned in a male body or vice versa. Not so long ago, these people were condemned to spend their lives in deep despair, feeling confused over their identity. Again, the various religions have caused immeasurable suffering and damage over the centuries.

I'm afraid that religious belief—in glaring contrast to what is preached—has all too much to do with egotism and self-love. Many people succumb to fascination with religion only because they can't accept the fact that after death it's all over. So they'd like to believe in something, but not out of love of their neighbor—they just want to book a ticket for immortality. Hence it is no coincidence that the God of the Old Testament is such an angry and punishing God. We should be afraid of him. Thou shalt fear the Lord your God. Like people on a plane who are scared as hell about flying. Gratuitous fear is pure selfishness. As soon as the same people have solid ground underfoot again, they'll calmly watch as the planes fly past: now it's no problem at all—they're not the ones on board. That's why I don't think religions are any use at uniting mankind. Instead, they tend to sow hatred and enmity. They are based in large part on selfishness, fear-mongering, and mass suggestion, and these things have never brought people together—quite the opposite.

And here's where anarchy comes back into the picture. When I decided to venture out onto the political battlefield, there was just a vague impression floating in front of me, something that can be difficult to bring into focus, hard to explain and define. Everything in life is relative. The perfect system that has an answer to every problem and will put the world to rights just doesn't exist. Therefore, groups and organizations of all kinds—clubs, faith communities, political movements, and schools—try to create a structure to refine and develop the whole thing into a living organism. Unfortunately, this organism or this phenomenon tends always to focus on itself and turns into a blind and rigid self-worship. So this creature, this amoeba or whatever we want to call it, has no front eyes, as the amoeba can't look forward any more than it can look back. It can't see the other amoebas or make contact with them, since these too have eyes only for themselves. Viewed in this way, such systems are like the cells in our bodies. And just as a cell can catch a virus, our systems are also exposed to all sorts of threats. Naturally, they respond by defending themselves on the outside, and thus compensate for their weaknesses.

I am such a virus. I was already a virus when I was a child, I was a virus at school, and I am a virus in politics. I am a troll among human beings. I am an anarchist. Not because I believe anarchism to be the perfect system. But because the perfect system does not exist.

AND NOW?

What's our conclusion? What's it all about? What is essential and what is not?

Despite all the media hype, I really don't see myself as the founder of a new generation of politicians, and I've long stopped trying to cobble together some smart ideology for myself. Even as a small boy, I had an aversion to anything to do with contests and competition. I simply had no desire to be the best at anything. Not at playing football, not at dancing, and not at anything else. The true winner of the game for me is the one who has the most fun, and this is true not only in sport, but also in life. When I acknowledged my affinity for punk, this was a clear statement of my determination to break away from all that success-oriented, competition-fixated, performance-related way of thinking.

Life is mainly there for us to enjoy it and have as much fun as possible, but we have to become active ourselves and come up with a few ideas. It doesn't need to be breathtaking—it's enough if it's surprising. Something unplanned always goes down well, because real surprises are becoming increasingly rare.

If I actually believe in anything at all, it's democracy. Democracy is the key to a progressive society. I believe in direct democracy. More precisely: in direct digital democracy. The threat to democracy is the misconception that we just need a capable leader, and then things will be sorted. But there are no such top dogs, even if everyone else is afraid to take responsibility, or simply too lazy to do so. Let's face it: most of us much prefer to check out the latest episode of *The Walking Dead* than to traipse to some public meeting. That's just how it is.

The Internet has changed the world, and it is about to change democracy. The Internet made Obama President of the United States, and it set in motion the Arab Spring. If you hand people the right tool for latching on to active democracy in a quick, uncomplicated way, from their computers, then they will most probably do so. But even here there are a few stumbling blocks. For example, we can't let this become a gateway for lobbyists or big political organizations that want to exploit it to increase their power.

First and foremost we need to find ways and means to encourage citizens to participate and contribute their own ideas. How about, for example, if you linked participation with a kind of lottery and lured people in with one hundred, or even five hundred attractive prizes? One hundred iPods or something? After all, we've all filled in a questionnaire and answered a few dumb questions in the hope that our name will end up being drawn out of the lottery and we'll win a mobile phone or some such gewgaw.

I am eternally grateful that I have been able to get to know so many interesting and wonderful people because of my position, people I would otherwise never have met: Noam Chomsky, Yoko Ono, and John Ralston Saul, Oliver Sacks and Richard David Precht. All these people have influenced me and helped me see a few things with different eyes. Of course there are many more people I'd dearly love to meet, but unfortunately I haven't as yet had the opportunity to do so. One of them is Ira Glass—ideally in an interview with me for *This American Life*. The British documentary filmmaker Adam Curtis, too: I'd like to have a cup of tea with him some time, as I've always liked what he does. And then, of course, there's Banksy. I owe him one, as he once did one of his graffiti for me. I'm always ready to invite Banksy to the best vegetarian restaurant he's ever been in. I know who he is, but I'd never breathe a word about it, or contact him on my own initiative. Banksy and I are in fact secret brothers. Okay, maybe not in a biological sense, but we are made of the same material. People like him, interesting, smart, and inspiring, these are the people with whom I want to spend my time. With people like that, I don't have to first explain what really counts, or tell them that you can't behave like an idiot when dealing with others. With these people I can always do business: we can build something up together, as that's what they want, too.

And that brings us back to the Best Party—because

here we have the essence of what it represents, what it wants and what it can do. Whether we can set up anything lasting, or really get things moving, remains to be seen. But at least we're still having just as much fun, and I think we've earned it.

I want to have fun, amaze other people, and amuse my audience, but never at the expense of others, more at my own expense. Ultimately, life is a roller coaster ride, it goes up and down, in ever shorter intervals. Sometimes we fall into a deep black abyss only to be flung just as rapidly up again and rewarded with a magnificent view. This roller coaster ride doesn't always suit everyone equally. Some turn chalk white with fear and huddle back in their seats, others close their eyes, others yell their lungs off. And then there are those who sit back and relax and just enjoy the ride. I'm one of them.

If I had to name something for which I'm prepared to commit myself even more seriously and more intensively, it's peace work—even though commitment to peace, absurdly enough, seems to be a risky business. Quite a few of those who work for peace end up in jail or simply get killed. But no matter where I'm headed, whether I get to be president or minister, whether I travel the world or simply emigrate to some distant country—I'm firmly determined to have fun. And in the future I intend to carry on with the amazing, amusing, and disturbing.

THE END

I made the Best Party on my own terms. At the start, I thought of it as an idea with a beginning, a rise, and an end. I'd like to think the story has all the characteristics of a classic novel, including a happy ending where good wins and evil loses. It's not always like that in reality, though.

But the beauty of the Best Party is that it doesn't exist—it's just an idea.

We won our election because we didn't play by the rules. The party never developed a real ideology or membership. You can call yourself a member if you like. It's a bit like AA—just without the steps.

As you may have gathered by what has come before, I have no business making politics my career, and I never had any plans of staying in politics forever.

In late 2013, as the end of my term neared, the polls showed that I had a good chance of winning reelection—with 35 percent support for a second term. But as I thought over the idea of a second term, I realized that we shouldn't push our success. What we pulled off with the Best Party was a surprise party, a shock to the system. But you can't have a surprise party follow a surprise party, or repeat this infinitely. If you try, you'll just get a regular party where people mingle and have fun, and then it's nothing special.

I started to explain this to my colleagues. When you talk about the difference between a regular party and a surprise party, people understand.

I soon announced to the public that I wouldn't seek reelection.

Part of the reason this was an easy decision is that many of the people I involved in the party turned out to be good politicians. Some of the smartest formed a new party called Bright Future. It has rules and a manifesto and membership. It is what you might call a liberal democratic party, and it's now one of the biggest political parties in Iceland. We decided to merge the Best Party into Bright Future, and we all plan to support Bright Future in the upcoming municipal elections. And Bright Future has been having a lot of success in Iceland! In the April 2013 election, they won six seats in the parliament.

You can say the Best Party will continue to exist as it always has. Anybody can run with it. There is no copyright for it. Anybody can make a Best Party just like anybody can make a surprise party. It is invisible, but if you put your mind to it you can see it. Can you?

INSIDE ICELAND

A statement by Jón Gnarr posted on February 15, 2010, on the website of the Best Party.

Wherever I show up, the people show an ardent interest in our domestic policy. They all want to talk about the Best Party with me.

I remember, for example, a well-attended solidarity meeting in a small town in the north, somewhere near Akureyri. There I met a man who was leading a sheep on a leash. The animal behaved like a dog, following him at every step and obeying his commands—"Sit" or "Down!" It had even learned to gnaw on a bone. After I'd talked with the man for a while and answered the various questions he asked, I wanted to know why he took this sheep around with him. "Because I love it," he replied without hesitation. I understood immediately. The life of the people out there is so different from our life here in the city. We hang out in our chic offices, sipping latte macchiatos and making a few decisions as we do so, while the people out there drink beer and have dinner with their herds of animals. The people in the countryside, especially up round Akureyri, speak an Icelandic that you could hear throughout the country twenty years ago, and is now almost every-where extinct. What we take for granted is often com-pletely alien to them.

Once we organized an information evening in Húsavík, on the north coast of Iceland, to which a group of farmers from the Mývatn region, also in the north, had also traveled. But they hadn't come to learn about the Best Party—they'd apparently heard the news going the rounds in Mývatn that I owned an iPhone. And now they all wanted to see the phone and begged me to allow them to touch it. I handed it to one of them and encouraged him to phone home. It's a scene I will never forget. The man was so moved that tears were running down his face as he called his children who were standing barefoot, gap-toothed, and filthy in some dunghill. He must have felt he was calling his family from some distant future. He didn't understand that the thing was simply a mobile phone.

It was then I realized that we are all creatures of feeling. The people in the country are mostly simple folk and can't do much more than shovel manure and stroke their sheep, or slaughter them in order to get through the winter. But they have feelings, and there-fore they belong to us. We all belong together, no mat-ter where we live. The Icelandic sheep connects us. Even if no one knows his sheep as well as does this farmer. He lives with it, eats together with it, takes it into the mountains and goes swimming with it, sleeps with it in the stable, and is probably the only person who knows when its birthday is. And then we come and take away his sheep and eat it. We can't pay any attention to the feelings of some yokel, of course.

We start the day with a workout in the gym, rush to and from work, and on the way home just have to pop into the mall. Nevertheless, we mustn't forget our roots. My grandfather was one of these country rubes, just like the countless others that we could observe in their natural habitat on our Land Cruiser Tour. We honk like crazy and growl curses under our breath if they chug along at a snail's pace ahead of us on their prehistoric Ferguson tractors. And if we eventually overtake them, they stare at us perplexed and offended, because the stresses of modern life have not yet reached them.

The Icelandic sheep is our secret emblem. It fills our bellies and keeps us warm. For us, it's like the bread and wine for the apostles at the Last Supper. We divide the world up by the color of its wool, and simply plod along behind the bellwether. And if the sheep could talk, it would ask us to be nicer to each other. No doubt about it.